POCKET MOM

Library of Congress Cataloging in
Publication Number: 2003096449

ISBN: 1-931686-83-1

Printed in Malaysia

Typeset in Bembo, Emmascript, and Franklin Gothic

Designed by Andrea Stephany

Illustrations by Carson Ellis

Distributed in North America by Chronicle Books
85 Second Street
San Francisco, CA 94105

10 9 8 7 6 5 4 3 2 1

Quirk Books
215 Church Street
Philadelphia, PA 19106
www.quirkbooks.com

POCKET MOM

EVERYDAY WISDOM,
PRACTICAL TIPS,
AND DOWN-HOME ADVICE

BY DINA FAYER

QUIRK BOOKS
PHILADELPHIA

Contents

Chapter 1: Good Habits

Chapter 2: Health and Hygiene

Chapter 3: Kitchen and Cooking Basics

Chapter 4: Housekeeping

Chapter 5: Love and Relationships

Introduction

Did you listen to your mother? Really listen? Sure, she sounded an awful lot like a font of wisdom—but she was still your *mom*. Which meant, of course, that no matter how smart she was, she knew *nothing*. About anything. (Or, at least, about anything important—like life and love and the right kind of shoes.)

More to the point, given the context of the fast-paced, modern world, you probably thought that no one could be *wronger* than Mom. After all, her advice was long past its expiration date, wasn't it?

Nothing could be further from the truth. If only you'd paid enough attention to Mom, you would know how good her advice always was—and still is. Mom was right. Mom is *always* right.

How she knows what she knows is a mystery, but what makes her unique is not that she can tell you how to clean a bathtub, but that she can tell you how to clean it *and* tell you why you're going to catch a cold if you don't wash your hands *and* explain why your last relationship was doomed from the start.

These days you may live far away from Mom. But have no fear: *Pocket Mom* is your one-stop reference for whenever you need a healthy dose of Mom (although of course there's no replacing the real thing). If you tuned her out the first time, this concise guide gives you a second chance to listen to her wisdom and advice, with easy instructions on everything from adopting good habits, to basic housekeeping, to what to do with a broken heart. It's Mom at her most infuriating best, with the convenience of one added feature— it's a book. You can shut it whenever you want . . . but gently.

Chapter 1: Good Habits

Mom is in the details. And as every Mom knows, the only way to make sure that all the details of life are taken care of is to adopt habits that will keep you operating at peak performance, all the time. Good habits improve your life and prevent the worst from happening: they are what stand between you and chaos. Here are Mom's best gems of advice to start you off on the right foot.

You Always Have Time to Tidy Up

Don't have time to put it away? Do it anyway. Right now.

Nice, clean surfaces are places where you can do stuff. Cluttered surfaces are places where you cannot. So every inch that's consumed by detritus is an inch where you can't get the job done—whether it's schoolwork, bill paying, or cooking a one-course meal. What's more, every urge to get the job done will be thwarted by the fact that you can't start anything before undertaking a major excavation.

If you want to change your habits, start now. Admit that

Moms and anal roommates aren't the only ones who take neatness seriously and make it something you care about. Then, try redefining *mess*. Mess isn't just the tools you leave out when a project is finished. Mess is anything left out of place, away from its home, or open—like uncapped toothpaste or a kitchen drawer. If it has to be moved at all, it's a mess.

Cleaning up is easy. The real trick is learning to *see* a mess—not the tenth or the fifth or the third time you step around it, but the very first time you lift your foot. It'll save you steps in the long run . . . and it'll save your relationship with anyone with whom you share living space.

If you aren't a fan of continuous cleanup, you've got some bad habits to break. There is *always* time to pick up after yourself, and unless you're about to dash from the house, there's time to do it immediately.

MOM SAYS: "Learn the basics of continuous cleanup."

1. Wipe the kitchen counters down after you've prepared a meal or snack. Brush errant crumbs into your hand, then follow up

with a quick swipe with a wet sponge to dislodge any other food particles.

2. Shift clean dishes from the dish rack directly into the proper cupboards before you wash your dirty dishes.

3. Always aim to wash your dishes right after your meal, or at least within the next two hours.

4. Take a quick pass at your sink with your sink hose so that stains and food particles don't build up.

5. Sort magazines and papers into "old" and "new" piles: place your old materials into the recycling bin and neatly stack the new stuff in a designated rack or table.

6. Hang up clothing before going to bed.

7. Put shoes away in closets or other designated shoe storage areas.

8. Straighten sofa cushions and throws before you leave for the day.

9. Empty ashtrays and throw away take-out containers as soon as you've finished with them.

There's a Place for Every Thing,
or How to Keep Track of Your Keys

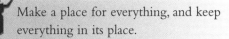

Make a place for everything, and keep
everything in its place.

Occasionally, losing your car keys can ruin your life—or
seem to, at the very least. You miss the interview and don't
get the job. You miss the audition and don't get the part.
You're late for a date and don't get . . . Well, you get the
point. You're being sabotaged by your lifestyle.

Establishing a home—both
handy and logical—for the
items you use every day
will help you remember
where to put things at
night, and where to
look for them in the
morning. No more
panic, no more tearing
the house apart.

Good Habits

Mom Says: "Tidiness is habit-forming."

1. No matter how tired you are in the evening, don't leave your coat unhung. Put it in the closet or on the coat rack as soon as you enter your home.

2. Get in the habit of putting your keys in the same spot each time you enter your home: on a mantel, on a side table, or—ideally—on a specially designated key hook, located near the front door.

3. Always place your purse or wallet in the same place—an entry-way table, coat rack, or desktop—as soon as you enter your home.

4. Sort and stack mail into desktop trays for bills to be paid, other communications requiring a response, and items to be recycled.

Being—and staying—organized affects your quality of life, whether you like it or not. Refuse to be neat, and you'll find yourself trapped in a strange, twilight adolescence—encumbered by mess and piles of old bills, and wondering what went wrong.

> *Tip* **If you have to leave your pants on the floor, be sure not to leave your keys in your pants!**

Make Your Bed Every Morning

You should always dress your bed for success.

Why should you make your bed? It always seemed like a pointless rule, especially when Mom insisted. But the truth is, abandoning your unmade bed is like leaving the night unfinished. Even if no one else sees your bed, *you* do—and you owe it to yourself to make your bedroom as welcoming and fresh when you return to it at night as you found it the night before.

A successful, happy lifestyle requires a certain amount of attention to the smaller details of life. Making your bed is just as important as tying your shoes or combing your hair before you go to work. Neglect those tasks, and you're not putting your best foot forward.

MOM SAYS: "Making your bed is quick and painless."

1. To start with, keep your bedclothes simple: choose one quilt or comforter that will serve as your bedspread; choose

durable but soft cotton sheets (the higher the thread count, the better, depending on your budget); choose comfortable pillows that give you proper neck support (remember to choose hypoallergenic fills if you suffer from allergies; otherwise, nothing beats a feather down).

2. Make your bed at a time that works best for you: As soon as you get up? After you've showered? Once you're dressed?

3. Now smooth out the creases in your fitted bottom sheet and tighten the sheet at its four corners.

4. Pull up your top sheet so that it is aligned with the top edge of the bed.

5. Now fold back the finished border of the sheet so that it fits snugly beneath your pillows.

6. Shake out your quilt or comforter and square it with the bed's four corners. You can leave the quilt squared with the edges or fold back the top edge to meet the top sheet.

7. Top it all off with your freshly plumped pillows and add a few colorful throw pillows if you have them. (Stuffed animal optional.)

Tip | **Reward yourself for keeping things tidy—buy yourself some flowers or some new art for your bedroom walls.**

Floss!

Flossing each day keeps the periodontist away.

You know you should. And sometimes, you even do it. But do you know how much you'll pay in 30 years (or less), if you don't? Refer to the chart on page 18 for some sobering statistics. But first, let's review the basics of floss.

MOM SAYS: "Thorough flossing takes only minutes a day."

1. Tear off an 18-inch (46-cm) length of floss from your floss dispenser.

2. Wind about 8 inches (20 cm) of floss around the middle fingers of each hand.

3. Hold the floss between your thumbs and index fingers, leaving a 1- to 2-inch (2.5– 5 cm) length in between. (As you floss, be sure to unroll a clean section of floss for each tooth—don't skimp!)

Good Habits

4. Use your thumbs to direct floss between upper teeth.

5. Use your index fingers to guide floss between the lower teeth.

6. Guide the floss up and down against the tooth surface and under the gumline.

The Costs

These numbers are the average cost of each of the most common periodontal procedures, after your insurance company has paid its share. If Mom couldn't convince you to take care of your gums, this sure-as-shootin' should.

Periodontic cleaning and scaling: $135
X-rays (full mouth): $150
Root canal (each tooth): $1,000
Porcelain crown (each): $1,000–1,500
Tooth extraction, first tooth: $570
Each additional tooth: $240
Periodontal full mouth scaling and root planing: $1,100
Osteosurgery: $1,100–1,400; add $500 for a bone graft

Single dental implant: $3,000; add $2,000 for crowns

Full mouth restoration:
Initial wax full mouth impressions: $1,100
Transitional crowns: $500 per tooth x 28 = $14,000
Permanent crowns: $1,000–1,500 per tooth x 28 = $33,600

Laugh at Yourself

When something goes wrong, don't chuck
something across the room; try chuckling, instead.

Learn to laugh at your own foibles and you will have a
lifelong skill that will carry you through every situation—
whether you're alone or in the company of family, friends,
and perhaps especially your partner.

In order to do this, you have to keep things in perspective.
Unless you're getting a liver transplant, an IRS audit, or a
divorce (or anything else that's similarly and actually horrific),
nothing is as important as it seems once
you've gained a little perspective.

Take your problems with all of
that stuff that just doesn't work
right. How many times have you
erupted at your computer, or
unloaded on your CD player, or
nearly broken your hand on the
steering wheel of your car? Catch
yourself next time you do it. Step
back and listen to the creative
stream of expletives screamed at full

volume at an inanimate object. When you stop, listen carefully: do you hear all that giggling? It's coming from the room next door. Someone is laughing at your reaction—and why? Because it's absurd. It's really funny. And if you think for a minute, you might even find yourself laughing, too.

Don't blame others for your own discomfort. No one is trying to make you feel like an idiot—so there's no need to puff up and get excited.

Sure, it's easy to laugh at other people, but once you relax, it's even easier to laugh at yourself. Be your own best audience. If nothing else, it means that someone is getting your jokes.

Don't Wait till the Last Minute

Never put off till tomorrow what you can do today.

Does this scenario sound familiar? There are 364 days before Christmas every year. That's a lot of time to shop. But you're always frantic the day before, and if the stores close too early, you're out of luck.

Or try this one: Your big report is due in two months, and you're eager to show off your stuff. But two months is plenty of time to write, so you don't have to start it right now. Three movies, four parties, and four hangovers later, you still aren't feeling creative . . . in fact, you might be getting a cold. So you read a book, instead. And finally, you're left with only a week to complete 20 pages of genius. But with so little time, how good can it be? Not as good as it could have been, that's for certain.

So why do you do it? Usually, the tasks you don't do right away are the ones you know you won't like. But putting them off doesn't make them go away, and it certainly doesn't make them more fun. Instead, it makes them more *unfun*, as well as stressful and darned near impossible.

If this is how you handle most things, you're either hooked on adrenaline or very, very tired. It isn't easy to thrive in a constant state of emergency. Procrastination isn't a choice; it's a compulsion.

Like any bad habit, this one is hard to kick, especially without a 12-step program. But grit your teeth and do it now.

MOM SAYS: "There's no time to waste on waiting."

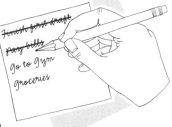

1. Recognize the thought patterns that make you procrastinate to begin with.

Is it anxiety about getting the job done properly? Are you not sure how to begin? Are you concerned that you're not going to do a perfect job of it?

2. Once you've figured out what's been holding you back, remind yourself that you've done plenty of hard tasks before. Remember how rewarding it was when you got the job done at last? Focus on your successes, not your failures.

3. Make a list of your priorities. Look at the calendar and sketch out a realistic timeline for the job. Divide up your working days into "dealable" chunks of time and smaller tasks, then pencil in each task in an individual block. (Always use a pencil so you can feel free to revise your list once the job is under way!)

4. Make your work environment as efficient and comfortable as possible (but not too comfortable). This means proper lighting and a neat work surface, if you're doing work at home. Be sure all the tools you need are immediately at hand so you don't have an excuse to get up and break your rhythm.

5. Reward yourself after you complete a task. First, cross the task off your timeline list—there's nothing more satisfying. Then choose your treat: a night out with friends? a trip to the gym? a hot (or cold) cup of your favorite beverage? You earned it!

Always Know What You Have in the Bank

A balanced checkbook means a balanced mind.

Do you know where your money goes? Try keeping careful track of your spending for one week. You might be surprised by how much you really spend on Starbucks (and other exotic liquids), plus snacks, entertainment, and assorted leisure activities. The good news is, budgeting doesn't mean you have to stop doing or buying your favorite things. You just have to plan for them.

MOM SAYS: "Realistic budgeting pays off in the long run."

1. Calculate your total monthly income to the exact decimal point.

2. Calculate the average total of monthly bills (rent, gas, electric, water, car insurance, phone, groceries, drugstore necessities, etc.) and deduct it from your monthly net income. The remaining sum is the most you can spend on leisure in a month. (If you frequently overspend, you might be the victim of an escalating habit. Pinpointing the problem and nipping it in the bud *now* will save you a lot in the end.)

3. Before you start spending all of your leisure allotment, deposit 10 percent of each paycheck into a savings account, preferably

one with a high interest rate. Since interest rates change daily, you'll want to poll the rates of several banks to find your best deal. And don't forget to research their policies on minimum balance and withdrawal to make sure you won't be assessed any penalties. It's convenient to locate your checking and savings accounts at the same financial institution, but do some comparison shopping online to make sure you aren't passing up an opportunity to earn more.

4. Manage your checking account. Don't leave it up to luck and the bank! Memorize your checking account number and your bank's account information phone number. Before writing any checks or using your debit card, call this number to determine your balance. Then, compare the current balance against your most recent hard-copy bank statement to see which transactions have posted to your account. Always log in each and every check you write, and always compare your checkbook balance against your bank statements, checkmarking the canceled checks as you receive them.

5. Keep your receipts and all written records of electronic transactions. If you're close to emptying your account every month, you can't afford to make expensive mistakes.

Your Not-Always-Current Balance

If you frequently use your debit card, do not take the balance information from the bank's phone line as gospel. Your "current balance" might not reflect every recent transaction.

Why? Your debit card purchases are electronically received by the bank on the same day you make them and then deducted from your account. But the next day—or days, depending on mail time—that purchase enters a strange, fiduciary limbo: the money may even magically reappear in your account. That's because, until your signature arrives at the bank, the transaction hasn't technically occurred, and the money hasn't left your account. At any time, one or more of your recent purchases could be stuck in limbo, and unreflected in your balance.

The best way to deal with this uncertainty is to tally all transactions that may not yet have been posted and leave yourself a healthy cushion to guarantee a positive balance.

6. Never, ever bounce a check. It will haunt your credit rating for years and leap out whenever you're ready to make a major purchase. Once you've got a bad credit rating, nothing is easy.

7. Pay all your bills (i.e., write checks or have funds electronically transferred) at the same time each month. This will help you keep a dependable, rough-and-ready estimate of how much you have left to play with in your account. You won't run out of

funds before a random bill comes due—and you won't be stuck with late fees and a blemished credit history.

8. Run a credit report once a year. Face the music, no matter how painful it is to hear (and pay for). A credit report will help you contain whatever damage you've done, adjust your budget accordingly, and, best of all, quickly identify any purchases made in your name through identity theft. The best way to combat this particularly nasty sort of fraud is to stop it as soon as possible, before it causes irreparable damage to your credit.

Tip | If you're sure identity fraud could never happen to you, think again. You know those preapproved credit offers that come to your house—the ones you have no intention of ever applying for? A dastardly sort of person could rummage through your recycling, put together the pertinent info, and be approved for all of that credit in your name. All of the purchases would be billed to your name—but of course you would never know until the credit card company tracked you down for nonpayment. If you work very hard and persevere, you could straighten out the damage . . . in a couple of years. A much better approach: Get yourself a cross-cutting shredder, and get into the good habit of destroying those offers as soon as you open them.

Always Keep a Map and a Flashlight (and More) in Your Car

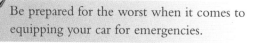 Be prepared for the worst when it comes to equipping your car for emergencies.

Mom always seemed to think that *everything* bad could happen to you the moment you got your driver's license. You'd nod and smile while she fretted over whether you'd stocked your glove compartment with a flashlight, checked your spare tire, or knew how to use a flare.

Of course, despite nodding and smiling (and eye rolling) your way through your teens, you had no intention of doing anything your Mom advised. And that's a shame. Proving Mom right by proving you're wrong can be painful, especially when you're stuck in the middle of nowhere in the middle of the night, trying to change a flat tire in the dark.

These days the cell phone is the device dearest to Mom's heart. It's the most important thing to keep in the car, especially if you're driving at night on unfamiliar roads. But having a map and a flashlight never hurts—and neither do a few of Mom's other helpful suggestions.

MOM SAYS: "Make sure your car is well supplied at all times."

1. **Tissues.** Keep those little packets in your glove compartment and you'll be amazed by how much tissue you go through in a week. They're especially handy when you don't get napkins at the drive-through; when you get gasoline on your hands; and when you have a deposit of film on your windshield.

2. **Flares.** They always seemed like such overkill—but if you ever have problems on a highway at night, you'll really want people to notice you. Carefully follow the directions printed on the wrapper. Generally, you'll remove the cap and use it as a striker to light the flare like a match, but read the instructions to make sure your particular flare isn't idiosyncratic. Three flares are ideal for alerting other motorists: place them about 20 feet (6.1 m) apart, starting directly behind your vehicle and working backward. If you have only one flare, put it 20 to 30 feet (6.1–9.2 m) behind your car.

3. **Tire repair gear.** Your gear should include a standard jack, a tire inflator spray can, and a spare tire (and a spare shirt, while you're at it). Be sure you're familiar with the tire-changing basics—if you haven't already learned to change a tire, ask a trusted friend or your friendly neighborhood mechanic to give you a quick lesson.

4. **Jumper cables.** You never know when or where you're going to end up with a dead battery, so it's worth your while to buy jumper cables. (Most tow companies charge at least $40 for coming out to jump your battery, and the kind person who

stops to see if you're okay might not have a set of her own.)

5. **Trunk stuffers.** Windshield-wiper fluid, motor oil, transmission fluid, and an empty gas can are always good things to have in your trunk. Be sure also to tuck away a first aid kit containing pain relievers, scissors, gauze, medical tape, disinfectant, burn ointment, adhesive bandages in various sizes, a vacuum-packed thermal blanket, and a couple of survival wafers. (You can purchase these kits at virtually any automotive supply store or one-stop franchise superstore.) Add a couple of bottles of water, and you've got all the basics.

Voilà! You're driving a Mom-car. It's not so bad, is it?

Tip | When driving in the winter or in rugged mountain terrain, keep rain or cold weather gear handy, plus snow chains, an ice scraper, a collapsible snow shovel, a battery-operated radio, and antifreeze.

Good Habits

Take a Seat When You Eat

Food that's savored is always more savory.

You eat while you walk, you eat while you stand, you eat in the car, and you eat while you're lounging in bed. But when was the last time you sat down at home for a meal? Not on the sofa, watching TV—but in an actual chair, at a table? If you have to take a minute to think, it's probably been too long.

Unlike Mom, you're probably pretty casual about food and feeding habits. Which isn't to say that you *forget* to eat, exactly, but that regular meals aren't a priority. And most of the time they aren't even possible—you're just too busy to care.

When you go to a restaurant and sit down to eat, it feels like a special occasion. Sitting in one place long enough to consume several courses, while nothing is flashing or beeping or distracting you from your meal, is a refreshing change of pace. The question is, why not do it more often?

You have the capacity to make your home dinnertime as special as a night out. Indulge yourself—buy a tablecloth! Or a nice set of napkins—why not? Pour yourself some sparkling water in a special wine glass. Take out the real dishes—not your paper take-out kind—and set a place setting. Then just pull up a chair, ignore the telephone for a while, tune out the outside world, and eat your dinner in peace (see pp. 91–99 for some sample dishes). You can save the sofa-loafing for dessert.

| Tip | Casual grazing is a wonderful way to consume calories without all the bother of thinking about it. But it's also a way to forget about health, which you need on your side when you're stressed. Protein shakes and energy bars aren't truly viable nutrition when you use them in place of meals, whatever their labels proclaim. No matter how much of it you eat, you can't look to snack food to save you. Try to make the most of your meals by cooking up some easy, balanced recipes. You and your body will be much happier in the long run. |

Chapter 2: Health and Hygiene

From tetanus shots to toenails, Mom has an angle on every aspect of your physical well-being. In this chapter we'll review all of the nagging insights and suggestions that used to make you seethe. Do you really need to wash your hands obsessively to fend off a cold? Are vitamins really that necessary? Is chicken soup really as good as penicillin? Is Mom's advice really as good as the doctor's?

Or is it really better?

Take Your Vitamins

> If you don't have time to eat right, be sure to take a multivitamin every day.

For many years, the potential benefits of vitamin supplements were regarded with distrust by the medical community. Some doctors wrote them off as wishful thinking, while others shrugged and figured they couldn't hurt. But Mom really seemed to believe those Flintstones chewables would keep you healthy. The fact is, Mom was right, particularly when you look at what passes for nutrition in today's fast-paced world of fast food and fad diets.

Researchers still say that if you eat a balanced diet, you probably don't need a supplement. But the difference between a recommended "balanced diet" and reality can be vast, no matter how hard you try to eat healthfully. And unless you're a monk or an athlete, there's bound to be at least one element in your lifestyle that depletes your body of nutrients. Drinking, smoking, taking aspirin or anti-inflammatories, and being pregnant can all take a toll and increase your need for supplements. But which one should you take?

MOM SAYS: "Read your labels and choose a vitamin that gives you the most of what you need."

1. The antioxidants—vitamins C and E—are the most important compounds to keep in your system, because they combat free radicals (ionized molecules that can damage cells and lead to cancer); your supplement should contain 250 to 500 milligrams of C and 200 to 800 international units of E.

2. Six to 15 milligrams of beta-carotene are also helpful—but only if you don't smoke. For unknown reasons, beta-carotene increases the risk of lung cancer for smokers.

3. Be sure your supplement contains the recommended dosages of vitamin A (180 micrograms), iron (15 milligrams), and calcium (the more the better, up to 2,500 milligrams). If you're pregnant, you should make sure you're getting enough folic acid.

Generally, manufacturers are careful to ensure that the quantities of vitamins, minerals, and polysyllabic compounds packed into each of their multivitamins do not exceed safe dosages. But beware of megadoses! Vitamins A and D can be toxic in large amounts, and niacin can also produce serious side effects. Excessive calcium consumption can lead to the formation of kidney stones and limit your body's absorption of iron, zinc, and other important elements.

Believe the Expiration Date

One of the crucial differences between Mom's medicine cabinet and your own (besides her tube of hemorrhoid cream and your tube of acne medicine) is that all of her pills, bottles, and tubes have future expiration dates, while yours are nearly old enough to go to school.

How much do those dates really matter? If you take a vitamin that's six months past the expiration date, will it work? Will it hurt you? Chances are, yes—it will work. And no—it won't hurt you. But that's just a vitamin. Take a course of expired antibiotics, and you could be in serious trouble.

Most drugs have a lifetime that exceeds their expiration date by months, if not years. But legally speaking, once that date has passed, you're taking that pill at your own risk. Manufacturers are required to certify their products as safe and potent only for the amount of time specified on the label, and most drugs aren't tested for longer than a year or two. Their effects after greater lengths of time are simply unknown.

So when your medicine cabinet gets crowded, it's probably time to weed out the oldsters.

Storing drugs in the bathroom is the worst thing you can do for their potency. Many drugs lose potency when they are exposed to heat and moisture, and bathrooms tend to be the hottest, dampest rooms in the house. Ideally, you should store your prescriptions someplace cool, dark, dry, and out of the reach of children—like a high closet shelf.

Grapefruit Gunpowder

Here's something Mom probably doesn't know: Never take drugs with grapefruit juice. In fact, doctors advise against taking some prescription drugs within *three days* of drinking grapefruit juice.

Whether it's fresh, frozen, or extra-pulpy, grapefruit juice contains several compounds that affect the way your body absorbs medication. When combined with a number of common prescriptions, a single 8-ounce (236-ml) glass of juice can increase a drug's rate of absorption and make it dangerously powerful. Adverse reactions range from serious to life-threatening, depending on the drug. So if you're ever medicated for anxiety, depression, high blood pressure, HIV, arrhythmia, infection, psychosis, high cholesterol, or erectile dysfunction, stay clear of grapefruit juice.

Germ Warfare, or How to Keep Your Hands Clean

Always wash your hands before coming to the table.

As it turns out, Mom's advice about clean hands is even more far-reaching than she knew. Ever take the bus? The train? The subway? If you don't hold onto the handrails, you're going to end up in someone's lap. But every time you enter a public domain, particularly when it has wheels and moves erratically, you're putting your hands where thousands of hands have gone before.

Colds travel from person to person by way of coughing, sneezing—and your fingers: whenever you scratch your eyes or your nose, you run the risk of introducing a whole menu of viruses into your system. And once the virus gets into your upper nasal passages, there's no way to avoid it. You're going to catch that cold.

In fact, your fingers are potential vectors for hundreds of air- and fluid-borne contagions, ranging from influenza to conjunctivitis to tuberculosis, especially in high-risk zones, like hospitals, commercial airliners, or preschools. (TB is one of the most common infections worldwide: According to the U.S. Labor Department, nearly one-third of the global population is already infected.)

MOM SAYS: "An ounce of prevention is worth a max-pak of tissues."

1. Wet your hands with warm running water.

2. Thoroughly lather your hands with antibacterial soap, rubbing your hands together for about 10 seconds (without water).

3. Lather the fronts and backs of your hands and between your fingers.

4. Use warm running water to thoroughly rinse your hands.

Tip | Wash your hands when you get off the bus or after you use a public phone or communal computer keyboard. Wash your hands before you dig into that order of French fries. If you're addicted to drive-throughs and eating on the run, it's a good idea to keep antibacterial lotion or towelettes in the car at all times.

Getting Cold and Getting a Cold

Bundle up or you'll catch a cold!

Mom got lucky on this one. There's no direct relation between catching a chill and catching a cold, but some peculiarities of the virus's lifestyle do make it look that way.

Despite the cold virus's hardy efficiency when it sets up shop in your system, it's a fragile creature when it's on its own. More than 200 viruses are known to cause colds, and the life span of each depends on what time of year it's set free in the world. Rhinoviruses (it's not too hard to guess what part of the body they affect) cause about one-third of all adult colds, and they thrive best during early fall, spring, and summer. The majority of colds, however, trace their lineage to several winter-loving families of bugs that are most active during periods of low humidity—also known as "cold snaps."

So one reason why people tend to catch cold when it's cold out is simply because there are more colds to be had. And Mom was right about not forgetting to wear your mittens—remember, the fewer germs your fingers pick up, the less likely it is that you'll convey those germs to your mucous membranes.

Wrap up well when it's cold outside, because bugs are likely to be flourishing; and wrap up well when it isn't even chilly—you'll make Mom feel better.

Could It Be Sinusitis?

Take care that your cold doesn't turn into a more serious infection.

Sinusitis is one of the most common ailments around, especially if you happen to live in an urban area where buses burp exhaust in your face and where air quality is generally poor. Despite the fact that its symptoms often seem more irritating than dangerous, sinusitis can be extremely damaging if left untreated. In its acute form, a sinus infection often manifests as the last, lingering stage of a cold or flu.

MOM SAYS: "Be on the lookout for the symptoms of infection."

1. Your nasal drainage (i.e., snot) may turn green, yellow, or bloody.

2. Your head may begin to ache behind your eyes, nose, and forehead.

3. You may find that your infected nose *smells*—or rather, becomes smelly—on the inside, of odors like manure or dirty feet.

4. If left untreated, your acute sinusitis will generally develop into bronchitis.

5. Sinusitis may sap your immune system, leaving you more open to acquiring other illnesses.

6. If you're under a lot of stress, sinusitis can even lead to depression.

The symptoms of acute sinusitis can be treated with anti-inflammatories and decongestants, but if you really want to knock it out, you'll need a short course of antibiotics. You don't want to take any antibiotic more often than you absolutely have to, but there are several newish, next-generation antibiotics out there that target this bacterium specifically, and nearly exclusively—so you aren't diluting your body's response to a vital, systemically effective drug like penicillin.

Chicken Soup Revealed

Eat your chicken soup and you'll feel better in no time.

For at least 900 years, the healing properties of chicken soup have been noted, exploited, and regarded as weird by the medical community. The first documented use of chicken soup as medicine was in the twelfth century, when Jewish physician Moses Maimonides prescribed it to relieve colds and asthma, and the tradition has been going strong ever since.

In the 1970s doctors began to look into the whys and wherefores of chicken soup's curative potential and decided that it must have something to do with steam. But since this wasn't much better than concluding that the stuff was magic and leaving it at that, several studies have recently reopened the case.

Their findings have raised a few eyebrows. It turns out that chicken soup does indeed contain certain "druglike" agents that minimize inflammation. Apparently, the soup inhibits the tendency of certain white cells, called "neutrophils," to con-gregate—which means that your bronchial tubes don't get as swollen and you cough a lot less.

The reasons *why* are still a mystery. In one study, the soup was diluted 200 times and it still produced the same result. In another, various permutations of herbs and vegetables (parsnips? sweet potatoes?) were added to determine their effect on the mix, and they made absolutely no difference at all. In fact, chicken soup straight out of the can seemed to be just as good at slowing white cells.

So while the medical community scratches its head and clears its collective throat, Mom gets another chance to use her favorite phrase: "I told you so!"

While off-the-shelf soup might have the same medicinal properties, it certainly doesn't taste as good as soup brewed up from scratch. So if your cold symptoms don't have you flat on your back already, get yourself a chicken.

Between the ginger, the curry, and the magical properties of chicken stock, your sniffles don't stand a chance.

Mom's Extra-Zesty Chicken Soup

Makes 4 servings

- 1 small chicken (broiler/fryer), cut up in chunks
- 1 teaspoon (5 ml) salt
- 1 teaspoon (5 ml) curry powder
- $1/2$ cup (185 g) ginger root (sliced or coarsely shredded)
- $1/2$ cup (185 g) rice (white or brown), uncooked
- 3 large carrots, sliced
- 1 medium-sized onion, sliced or julienned
- 3 stalks celery, chopped
- $1/2$ teaspoon (2.5 ml) pepper

1. Place the chicken in a large pot, and pour enough water in to cover the chicken.

2. Add salt, curry, and ginger.

3. Bring the water to a boil; continue boiling for 30 minutes or until chicken begins to fall off the bone.

4. Remove the chicken from the pot.

5. Let stock cool in refrigerator until the fat rises to the top.

6. Skim off the fat with a spoon and remove the ginger.

7. Shred the chicken and add it to the cooled stock along with rice, veggies, pepper, and another pinch of salt. For extra zing, add another pinch of ginger root, finely grated.

8. Bring the soup to boil and continue boiling for 30 minutes, or until fork–tested vegetables are cooked to your satisfaction and the rice is done.

More Comfort Cures from Mom

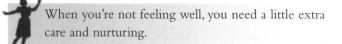 When you're not feeling well, you need a little extra care and nurturing.

Chicken soup isn't the only weapon in Mom's arsenal. The next time you're feeling punky, try one of these time-tested cures.

MOM SAYS: "Small comforts reap big rewards."

For a quick recovery (from feeling drained or run-down): *Gingersnap milk*. Shred a small piece of ginger and add it to a (microwave-safe) cup of milk (or soy milk). Add a spoonful of blackstrap molasses and heat in the microwave for about a minute, or blend care-fully in a pan on the stove-top until warm. Stir before drinking.

For congestion: *Ginger lemonade.* Steep 2 tablespoons (30 ml) of shredded ginger in a medium-sized pot of boiling water for several minutes, then allow the water to cool (or put it in the freezer for quick cooling). Squeeze fresh lemons, and add the juice to the water (one part juice to three parts water). Add a spoonful of honey or sugar to taste.

For sore throats: *Hot Jello.* Prepare a box of Jello, pour it into a mug, and drink it while it's hot, like tea.

For nausea: *Flat soda.* Allow soda of any kind to go flat at room temperature. Drink slowly, and chase with a glass of water.

For stressed-out skin: *Homemade healthy mask.* In a small bowl, combine several tablespoons (50 g) of dry clay with a squirt of aloe vera juice and a tablespoon (15 ml) each of red cider vinegar and blackstrap molasses. Stir briskly with a spoon or wooden stirrer until the mixture becomes moist and mudlike in texture. Spread a thin layer of mud on your face, and allow it to dry. Remove with a washcloth and warm water.

When Mom Is Not Enough: Time to Call the Doctor

If it's still there in two days, *then* worry about it.

Statistically, only a tiny percentage of headaches are caused by brain tumors or aneurysms. Fewer than 2 percent of odd-looking moles are malignant melanomas. Chest pain is, more often than not, indigestion, and heart palpitations are usually revealed to be esophageal spasms.

Every other day, it seems, you wake up with a blotchy patch of skin or swollen glands or persistent and inexplicable pains in your abdomen. It's probably nothing, but it could be deadly. So how do you know when to panic?

Wait two days. If the symptoms stop, you've saved yourself the agony of sleepless nights and condescending doctors. If they're still there after two days, it's time to schedule a visit to the doctor.

Warning: Do not delay seeing a doctor if the pain is sharp and focused in the lower right side of your abdomen—particularly if you still have your appendix.

> **Tip** | If you've got a particularly nasty headache, bend your head forward: If you're able to do so without increasing the level of pain, you're probably not suffering from anything more serious than a headache—and not, as you'd feared, an aneurysm.

Mom Says: "Do what the doctor tells you (most of the time)."

No one likes going to the doctor—it's like admitting defeat. But if your throat is sore and dotted with odd white patches, you may very well have strep—which over-the-counter remedies simply can't fix. And that persistent cough, which could be bronchitis or walking pneumonia, will hang around for a week if it's treated by a doctor, or three months if you stick with an expectorant.

As common as it is for patients to delay seeking professional help, doctors say that it's even more common for patients to show up, nod their heads as they listen to their advice, and then happily fail to take it.

So follow your doctor's directions—all of them, for as long as the doc says you have to.

1. Take your medication as directed—and make sure you understand whether the dosage is daily or "as needed."

2. If antibiotics are prescribed, finish the bottle. If that bacterium isn't completely annihilated, your illness can recur.

3. If you're uncomfortable with your doctor's recommendation, don't simply ignore it. Ask about alternative treatments.

4. Ask about the side effects of any drug prescribed.

5. Ask your doctor to be honest with you about the certainty of her diagnosis, especially when your symptoms are ambiguous.

Your last line of defense against uncertainty is research: It pays to learn about your condition and its potential solutions. If you need to read up on the history and vital statistics of a particular condition or to review research results, visit the on-line sites of any schools and organizations that are sponsoring research into your topic—look for the .edu and .org addresses as you flip through the index. The library is another treasure trove of information where you can pore though articles about your condition in the current and back issues of major science journals.

Tip | **Be aware that too much medical literature can give you a nasty case of the what-ifs, and hypochondria can make you sick!**

Never Double Up on Dosages

Here's one area where two are definitely not better than one. Your over-the-counter habits ("If one is good, two are better") are downright dangerous when applied to prescription drugs. If you double the dose of an antibiotic in order to finish the pills in half the time, the drug's effectiveness will be reduced by nearly half. Double the dose of a stimulant, and you run the risk of acute arrhythmia and heart attack. Double up on an anti-depressant, and you might produce a long-term neurochemical imbalance.

Here's another tip: No matter how well a drug works for you, don't give a few "extra" pills to a friend with similar symptoms. The antibiotic that dries up your bacteria-caused cough in two days may not have any effect on his cough because it was caused by a virus.

Get That Second Opinion

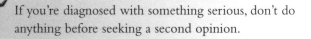 If you're diagnosed with something serious, don't do anything before seeking a second opinion.

Doctors are people, too—some are open to trying new methods, while others are resistant to change. If your life is on the line, you owe it to yourself to verify your diagnosis and to seek treatment options from several different sources. If your doctor's recommendation seems extreme, don't take it at face value. Take it as a vote, and don't select a treatment without polling someone else. Most health plans (even the worst ones) will cover a second exam if you're referred by your physician.

Mom Says: "Take the time to find the right specialist."

1. Ask your physician to recommend *several* appropriate experts. Some doctors have a you-bill-my-patient, I'll-bill-yours arrangement with one or more of their friends, and view referrals as opportunities for reciprocation. The second (or if necessary, the third) specialist your doctor recommends is more likely to be a professionally respected colleague than a personal friend, which means that his manner and perspective could be refreshingly different.

2. If face-to-face doctor-shopping sounds a bit stressful, contact your health organization and request a list of specialists in your area.

3. Visit Internet chat rooms and open forums that patients with your condition frequent, and start trading information with others. Patient referral is one of the surest ways to locate a specialist, because fellow patients generally share the same

fears, concerns, frustrations, and requirements. Only another patient can give you the real scoop on a specialist's communication skills, confidence, and bedside manner.

When Was Your Last Tetanus Shot?

Always keep your immunizations up-to-date.

Think back: The last tetanus shot you remember, you were probably dragged there by Mom, assaulted by a cheery nurse with a huge needle, and succored by a cherry-flavored lollipop. If you were lucky, it left a bruise for only a day or two. If you were really lucky, you got a sucker that wasn't broken. And that was the end of your anti-tetanus regimen.

As it turns out, though, it's a good idea to get a tetanus shot every ten years. Tetanus shots aren't like vaccines—they don't protect you for a lifetime. And you never know when your next encounter with a rusty nail or hungry spider will occur.

Tetanus is caused by an organism called *Clostridium tetani*, which is found in soils, manure, manure-enriched soils, and the digestive systems of creatures who crawl through manure. The tetanus spore enters through a puncture wound or bite and migrates through the central nervous system, causing spasms and rigidity of voluntary muscles (hence the nickname "lockjaw"). The mortality rate in humans is extremely high—from 40 to 80 percent of all those infected.

So, while there's little chance that an itchy bite will develop into full-blown tetanus, it's best to remember that little things can have big teeth (or fangs). Get the booster! Then you can scratch that itch without worry.

MOM SAYS: "Always keep track of your shots and immunizations."

You may not always have Mom around to remind you, so start taking responsibility for tracking your immunizations, allergies, and medical history as well as the common ailments you may or may not have been exposed to as a child.

	Date	Date	Date	Date
1. Hepatitis A				
2. Hepatitis B				
3. Measles				
4. Mumps				
5. Rubella				
6. Polio				
7. Diptheria				
8. Pertussis				
9. Tetanus				
10. Pneumococcal disease				
11. Varicella (chicken pox)				
12. Influenza				
13. Small pox				
14. Other				

Store this information, along with a list of statistics including your blood type, known allergies, and pharmaceutical sensitivities, in an expandable file marked "Medical History." Instead of discarding your prescription slips, put them in the file so you'll have an ongoing record of your treatments. Add a one-sheet summary of your parents' medical histories, including details on any hereditary diseases.

Whenever you register with a new doctor's office, ask your former physician to transfer your medical records to the new address. Your records should remain intact as they follow you from place to place, but just in case your old doctor loses your data, you should keep your own record of each visit to the doctor. Each entry should include the doctor's full name, phone number, and office/email address, the reason for your visit, the doctor's diagnosis, and a list of any additional procedures—including lab work and X-ray imaging.

Turn That Racket Down!

You'll damage your ears if you play your music too loudly.

The human ear evolved in a world without Dolby. Our sensitive auditory organs were designed, over millions of years, to pick up soft sounds—like animals breathing or twigs snapping—so you can't expect them to survive a daily barrage of Surround Sound unscathed

Prolonged exposure to noise can cause permanent hearing loss. A constant noise level of 85 decibels (about the level of a working microwave oven) over a period of 40 hours can be just as damaging as an hour of 100-decibel arena rock. So just imagine what your home stereo—and even worse, your Walkman—is doing to your poor little ears, every day.

Every individual suffers a different rate of aural decay, based not only on decibel doses but on genetic factors such as gender, eye color, and ethnicity. But once your hearing is gone, it's gone. Not even state-of-the-art hearing aids or cochlear implants can return every nuance of sound to damaged ears.

MOM SAYS: "You've got only one set of ears—you'd better take care of them."

1. If you're going to a show, bring a pair of foam earplugs. The music will be every bit as audible, and you won't miss the ringing in your ears afterward. (Be sure to follow the insertion instructions carefully.)

2. If you use a Walkman, turn it up no higher than level 2.

3. If you work in a factory or in construction, wear protective muffs. Loud industrial noises can be even

more damaging than ball-bouncing bass.

4. Try to avoid prolonged exposure to other loud sounds, including firecrackers and jet engine noise.

5. If you suspect you may have sustained some hearing loss, contact your doctor to schedule a hearing screening.

Wax Facts

If you won't turn down the volume, your earwax can do it for you. Earwax is in the sebum family—people with oily hair and skin produce a lot of it. (If your skin type is normal to dry, you're probably out of luck.) If you're of the oily ilk and are experiencing hearing loss or balance problems, it's probably time to clean your ears. Twice daily for several days, put one drop of warm oil (mineral or vegetable) into your ear canal, then irrigate the ear with warm water and let it drain. If this doesn't clear out the wax, see a doctor; the problem might not be wax related.

Servicing Your Toenails

Avoid ingrown toenails by buying—and wearing—sensible shoes.

Toenails aren't a critical part of your anatomy—until they become ingrown and have you hobbling from place to place, of course.

Ingrown toenails usually appear on your big toes, which you use to support and balance a surprising percentage of your body weight. So when that nail grows inward, it's pressed more deeply into the skin with every step you take.

Once it's reached that stage, there's no quick way to solve the problem. If it doesn't make you completely queasy, you can use tweezers to get under the nail, pry it from the tissue, and lift it up enough to slide a piece of cotton gauze underneath. You'll have to do this every day until the nail finally grows out past the problem.

If the tweezer trick is too painful to complete and the toe is actually tender to the touch, the nail is probably infected. Look for discoloration, swelling, or discharge. If your toe fits the profile, you should seek professional treatment. (If nothing else, a shot of anesthetic will make the trip worthwhile.)

MOM SAYS: "Prevention is key."

1. Be sure to cut your toenails regularly. If they get too long, they can split, break, and poke holes in the skin of neighboring toes (this is particularly painful if you're wearing tight shoes).

2. Always cut your toenails straight across—*do not* cut downward at the corners, into the cuticles.

3. If your toenails tend to be tough, take a shower to soften them up.

4. Cut each nail completely. If part of the nail is still attached when you pull it, keep cutting until it separates. (Don't just tear the thing off.)

5. Wear sensible shoes. Save all of those excitingly contoured, pointy-toed favorites for evenings or special occasions.

There's No Fun When It Comes to Fungus

One day, you're cutting your toenails (straight across), and your clipper appears to develop a problem. No matter how much you push and wiggle, you can't wedge your big nail between the clipper's teeth. What gives?

If this ever happens to you, don't blame it on the clipper. You've contracted toenail fungus. Thickening is a common symptom of the fungus, along with dryness, striation, and discoloration. Some sufferers experience nothing worse than a few white or yellow spots, while others end up with truly hooflike deformations that require maintenance, and sometimes removal, by a podiatrist.

It might sound like a biblical form of punishment, but don't flatter yourself that you've been singled out: Toenail fungus affects approximately 10 to 12 million people in the U.S. alone. Studies show that if your toes bang into the tips of your shoes often enough from jogging or skiing downhill, dancing on your toes, or working all day in tight shoes or steel-toe boots, you're at risk for developing the fungus.

Prevention is a matter of common sense:

1. Never use anyone else's clippers, and if you use the same clippers on your fingernails, disinfect them with alcohol first, letting them air dry for 60 to 90 minutes before their next use.

2. Check out your salon's disinfecting protocols before getting a pedicure.

3. Always wear clean socks.

4. Always try shoes on before you buy them to ensure a proper (not overtight) fit.

If you've already contracted the fungus, you don't have a lot of options, alas. You can either make it a part of your lifestyle, or you can pay a truly ghastly sum for a three-month course of oral antifungals. These drugs have a decent cure rate, but it will take more than a year to return toenails to their former pristine prettiness—and then there's a substantial chance that the fungus will recur. So take Mom at her word—prevention is worth it!

Chapter 3:
Kitchen and Cooking Basics

Is your kitchen zoned for comfort or combat? Do you cook your meals or nuke your rations? If "home cooking" means going to a friend's house for dinner, it's time for some basic insight from Mom.

For competent cooks, the following advice can serve as a refresher course with a few handy tricks thrown in. Want to whip practically nothing into something? Or how about a whole new menu of somethings? For novices, this chapter will introduce you to the one room of the house you have yet to conquer.

Treat your kitchen like a brave new world, and explore it! Mom will be so proud.

Anatomy of a Kitchen

The secret to a happy kitchen is keeping it clean and orderly.

More than any other room you inhabit, your kitchen has to be *organized*. If your tools are out of place, or if they don't have a place to begin with, you start every meal at a disadvantage. Ever wonder why some people love to cook while others shudder at the thought? Chances are, it's their kitchen setup that makes the difference.

Becoming—and remaining—organized may not be second nature to you, but once you've cooked (or tried to cook) in the midst of a mess, you know just how wearying disorganization can be.

The key is deconstruction. You may have been steeping tea and heating takeout in your kitchen for years—but when was the last time you opened the drawers? Or looked in the backs of your cupboards? Where did you stash the garlic press and the yolk separator (and what does one look like, anyway)?

Mom Says: "Before your kitchen can function properly, you have to know what's there and what you don't need."

1. Systematically remove the contents of drawers, cupboards, pantries, and spice racks and place it all on your countertops and/or kitchen table.

2. Corral any appliances that regularly live on the countertop (like coffee grinders and coffeemakers) in an out-of-the-way corner so that you have more organizational space.

3. Next, set out three cardboard boxes or paper bags. With a felt-tip pen, write "KEEP" on one box, "DONATE" on another, and

"TRASH" on the third.

4. Starting with your drawers, sort the contents into these three
boxes. Put one of each basic tool (see next page) into the
KEEP box, along with any other intact items. Usable, undam-
aged duplicates belong in the DONATE box, and all broken or
rusty tools go in the TRASH box.

Your Basic Kitchen Tools

Must haves:	Should haves:
Carving knife	Apple corer
Serrated knife	Garlic press
Spatula	Turkey baster
Slotted spoons	Pastry brush
Cheese grater	Frosting spatula
Measuring cups	Ladle
Measuring spoons	Strainer
Meat thermometer	Tongs
Can opener	Potato ricer
Corkscrew	Mandoline
Vegetable peeler	Yolk separator
Wire whisk	Funnel

Kitchen Prep School

The secret to easy, efficient food preparation is . . . more preparation.

If you begin your kitchen journey with a full supply of proper equipment, you'll save yourself a lot of time, trouble, and frustrated make–do effort. Here's a list of what you'll need:

1. **Cutting boards** (two). One board should be reserved for cutting vegetables and the other for chicken and meats. Plastic or glass boards are generally inexpensive and dishwasher-safe, but the old-fashioned wooden boards tend to be heavier and less likely to slip around.

2. **Mixing bowls** (three). Purchased as a set or as single items meant to be stored together, your small, medium, and large mixing bowls (metal or ceramic) should stack concentrically for easy storage. Keep them looking nice, and they can double as serving bowls in a pinch.

3. **Colander.** Plastic or metal, your colander should be large enough to strain a full pot of pasta or enough salad to feed four people.

4. **Kitchen timer.** An inexpensive digital or mechanical timer is ideal.

5. **Microwave-safe storage containers** (six)—in assorted sizes, with lids that fit. Nearly all plastic and glass dishes are microwave-safe. Metal containers of any kind should never be used in the microwave; if you're reheating take-out food, make sure that the takeout container doesn't have a metal handle.

6. **Storage canisters** (five or six). To prevent bugs from getting into your main ingredients, pour flour, sugar, coffee, cereals,

and other boxed or bagged staples into airtight storage containers. Purchase a simple, no-nonsense set (or several separates) for utilitarian purposes, or take the opportunity—if you've got the counter space—to show some style by displaying new or vintage decorative canisters.

7. **Baking supplies.** A rolling pin (Mom's wooden one is best; if you're worried about keeping it clean, wrap the roller in plastic cling-wrap each time you use it), a sifter, and a wire whisk are particularly useful; check your cookbooks to identify other necessary tools that might be worth the investment.

8. **Protective/safety items.** Stock up on trivets or pads to put beneath piping-hot pots and casserole dishes, and two or more potholders or oven mitts to protect your hands. To combat cooking fires, you should purchase a dry chemical or foam fire extinguisher that is approved for fighting electrical, grease, and flammable liquid fires.

Unstuffing Your Cookware Cupboard

It's time to drag out the heavy artillery.

Unless you're equipping a kitchen from scratch, your collection of cookware is bound to be a motley crew. You may have two or three pots of every size (and double the number of lids), an endless supply of frying pans, and a cupboard full of odd-shaped thingies, whose purpose is anyone's guess. Where do you go from here?

Mom Says: "Boil down your cooking supplies to the basics."

Here's what you need:

1. One 8- or 10-quart (7.6–9.5 L) stockpot with lid.

2. One 4- or 5-quart (3.8–4.7 L) pot with lid.

3. One 1- or 2-quart (1–1.9 L) saucepan with lid.

4. One large 10" or 12" (24–30 cm) heavy skillet—preferably one with a lid.

5. Three round or oval glass ovenware casserole dishes (with lids) in 1-quart, 1½-quart, and 2-quart (1, 1.4, 1.9 L) sizes.

6. Assorted baking pans: One bread loaf pan, one 9" x 9" (23 x 23-cm) square cake pan, two 9"(23-cm) rounds for layer cakes, one 9" x 13" (23 x 33-cm) rectangular cake pan, and one nonstick cookie sheet should be adequate for baking the basics. Your pans and cookie sheet should be sturdy enough to evenly conduct heat without warping.

Strategically stacked, your set of cookware should fit neatly into one cupboard—or two if your cupboards are small.

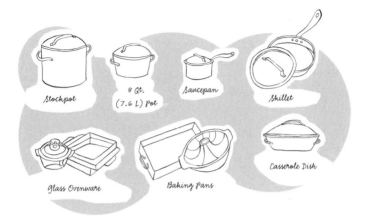

Stockpot

8 Qt. (7.6 L) Pot

Saucepan

Skillet

Glass Ovenware

Baking Pans

Casserole Dish

Tip | Critics and moms agree that stainless steel is the way to go if you're looking to invest in a good, durable set of pots and pans. Round out your set by purchasing one or two cast-iron skillets or saucepans. You won't use them every day, but there are some recipes for which nothing else will do.

The Joys of Shelf Paper

Clean shelves give you peace of mind.

Practically speaking, there are several good reasons for putting down paper in drawers and on shelves. Shelving or contact paper provides a clean surface for storing dishes and utensils and saves you from having to disinfect wood—which, since it's porous, is almost impossible to disinfect. At the same time, its vinyl or wax coating protects the wood from water damage, and you have only to wipe it down with a damp cloth once every few months and change it every couple of years to keep it tidy.

Shelf paper's net effect on your kitchen might be small, but its effect on *you* will be magical: As you're installing shelf paper, don't be surprised if it makes you suddenly really happy.

MOM SAYS: "Shelf papering your kitchen is a great way to start over."

Pick out paper that appeals to you and don't worry too much about committing to a color scheme; it's going to be hidden inside drawers and cupboards for the most part. Most hardware, discount, and general superstores stock several brands and styles of shelf paper, so you're sure to have plenty of options.

1. Wipe the grit from the drawer, cupboard, or shelf with a damp, soapy rag.

2. Without removing the sticky backing, unroll the paper and put it in place to check for sizing. If it's too wide, use a pencil to mark the correct width on one edge, then remove the paper and use a ruler to draw in the rest of the line. If the shelf is notched or oddly shaped, pencil in the notches or trace the entire shelf.

3. Following these lines, use scissors or a utility knife to remove the excess.

4. Now, lift the backing from the top and bottom corners of one side of the paper and stick the paper to the shelf (making sure that the corners of your paper are properly snugged into the corners of your shelf). Moving from this first side to the opposite side, remove the backing and stick the paper to the shelf.

5. Stroke the surface of the paper with firm pressure to smooth out the wrinkles.

6. Stand back and admire your handiwork.

Organizing Kitchenware: What Goes Where?

Organization is a matter of storing tools in their most logical places.

Your empty, shelf-papered drawers and cupboards are now ready to be filled. Most kitchens are designed with at least

four big drawers; if you're blessed with more, you can spread out your utensils or make a home for hot pads.

However you organize, remember the goal: you're planning to cook in this kitchen. If drawers are packed too tight, utensils can swim to the bottom and hide.

MOM SAYS: "Organized drawers and cupboards are next to godliness."

1. Invest in some drawer dividers to ensure the utensils don't become an unwieldy pile once they're stored. A plastic or wooden tray with individual slots for silverware is a must.

2. Assign one drawer for your silverware and put each piece in its designated tray slot.

3. Assign your most-used cooking utensils to another drawer, making sure that the drawer can still open and close easily once full.

4. Assign plastic storage bags, plastic wrap, and aluminum foil to a third drawer.

5. Assign emergency gear—flashlights, candles, batteries, and so on—to a fourth "utility" drawer.

6. Place drinking glasses on a low shelf, since you're likely to use these the most.

7. Similarly, store your most-used plates and bowls on a lower shelf that can be accessed easily and often.

8. Assign cups with handles to a middle shelf.

9. Place stemware on a higher shelf, where it won't be jostled.

Tip | **If you only use an item for special occasions (e.g., Mom-attended dinners), store it on the very top shelf of your cabinet or cupboard.**

Kitchen and Cooking Basics

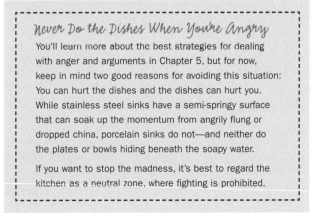

Never Do the Dishes When You're Angry

You'll learn more about the best strategies for dealing with anger and arguments in Chapter 5, but for now, keep in mind two good reasons for avoiding this situation: You can hurt the dishes and the dishes can hurt you. While stainless steel sinks have a semi-springy surface that can soak up the momentum from angrily flung or dropped china, porcelain sinks do not—and neither do the plates or bowls hiding beneath the soapy water.

If you want to stop the madness, it's best to regard the kitchen as a neutral zone, where fighting is prohibited.

A Place for Your Place Settings

A civilized meal begins with a dedicated place setting.

If you're living in a combined household, it's a good bet that your cupboards are full of collected oddments like commemorative mugs, sloganed shot glasses, and wobbly stacks of unmatched plates and bowls. But if four to six people at a time regularly sit down to meals together (or if your household tends to host a lot of parties), your stock of place settings should include eight to ten coffee cups or mugs, saucers, water glasses, wineglasses, dinner plates, bowls (small and large), and silverware settings.

If you're outfitting your kitchen from scratch, it's easiest to purchase a prepackaged assortment of place settings; these generally include six or eight cups, saucers, plates, and bowls. (Prepackaged silverware sets tend to contain a similar number of settings.) Water glasses and wine glasses can be purchased singly or in sets of two, four, or six—if you're on your own, start with four of each. And remember, it's always best to keep two spares of each kind of glass and dish available for contingencies.

MOM SAYS: "Don't forget the niceties when it comes to setting your table."

If you want to up the ante on your lifestyle and say good-bye to paper napkins, paper plates, and paper towels at every meal, try giving your dining room table some additional character and class.

1. Ready-made **tablecloths** are available in various standard sizes and a multitude of styles—and if you don't like what you see on the shelves, you can purchase the fabric to make your own. Be sure to check the care instructions before dropping any tablecloth into the washing machine, and prepare to do some ironing when it comes out of the dryer or off the clothesline if it's made of cotton or linen.

2. If you don't want to fuss with a tablecloth, try **placemats**. Purchase six or eight in a style you like, made of durable, washable fabrics. ("Dry clean only" placemats are wonderful for special occasions, but needlessly expensive on an everyday basis.)

3. Choose some nice **cloth napkins** to complete the picture. Remember to buy several more napkins than you think you need, because damage is inevitable and replacements are generally hard to find after a few years (or even months).

Tip | If you want to make your own placemats, choose a heavyweight cotton or linen. Two yards of 45"-wide (114-cm) fabric or one yard of 60"-wide (152-cm) fabric will make six double-sided placemats. For added flexibility, you can choose two complementary fabrics and sew them back-to-back to create reversible placemats.

To Chuck or Not to Chuck: Cleaning Your Refrigerator and Freezer

 Purge your refrigerator and freezer once a month to reduce clutter.

Mom knows it, and it's high time you learned it, too: Even refrigerated and frozen food will eventually go bad. Use the following guidelines for determining which things are "overripe" enough to merit disposal.

Refrigerator

Chicken (cooked): 3 days

Chicken (uncooked): 1 day

Fish (cooked): 2 days

Fish (uncooked): 1 day

Meat (cooked): 3–4 days

Meat (uncooked): 2 days

Condiments: once opened,
2 months

Juice: 2 weeks

Cheese: 3–4 weeks; 3–4 months
if stored in an airtight bag

Milk: 1 week; see use-by date

Butter: 2 weeks

Eggs: 3 weeks; see expiration date
on carton

Bread: 1 week, if fresh

Wine (unopened): dependent on quality and vintage

Wine (opened): 12 hours (white); 1 week (red)

Jam/jelly: 4 months

Cooked pasta: 3–4 days

Freezer

Fish: 6 months

Chicken: up to 1 year,
depending on packaging

Ground beef: 3 months

Frozen dinners/pizzas: 3–4 months;
see expiration dates on box

Ice cubes: 2–3 months or until
they develop a funny smell

Tip | **It's time to defrost the freezer when the kitchen develops air conditioning, courtesy of a freezer door that won't stay shut.**

Stocking Your Kitchen: The 33 Basic Ingredients

 Now that you've reclaimed your kitchen, it's time to stock the larder.

The question is, with what? There's a big difference between shopping for food to reheat and shopping for food to *cook*. On the following page, you'll find a list of 33 handy, versatile items to keep in your fridge, freezer, and pantry. These are baseline ingredients—the very least you need to start cooking at home. The possibilities are limitless. Just use your imagination (or refer to page 80 for some basic mealtime math for any time of day).

33 Basic Ingredients

Refrigerator	Freezer	Pantry
Eggs	Broccoli	Tuna
Milk	Sausage	Granola
Butter/margarine	Spinach	Pasta
Mayonnaise	Vanilla ice cream	Bread
Fresh tomatoes	Mixed vegetables	Bisquick
Fresh mushrooms	Chicken breasts	Maple syrup
Peanut butter	Ground beef/turkey	Rice
Cheese	Coffee	Potatoes
Mustard	Strawberries	Olive oil
Italian dressing	Juice (concentrate)	Stewed tomatoes
Lettuce	Cool Whip	Onions

Mealtime Math

Just add up the opportunities for these easy meals!

Breakfast

Milk + granola + strawberries = cereal

Eggs + milk + spinach + onions + sausage + olive oil = omelet

Eggs + bread + butter + maple syrup = French toast

Strawberries + juice concentrate + milk + whipped cream = smoothie

Lunch

Lettuce + tuna + tomatoes + Italian dressing = basic tuna salad

Cheese + bread + butter = grilled cheese sandwich

Ground beef + lettuce + onion + tomato + cheese = burger

Tuna + mayo + onion + bread + lettuce + mustard = tuna sandwich

Peanut butter + bread = fallback favorite

Dinner

Chicken breasts + egg + bread (crumbs) + cheese = chicken parmigiana

Ground beef + egg + bread (crumbs) + stewed tomatoes = meatloaf

Potatoes + cheese + olive oil = potatoes au gratin

Broccoli + mushrooms + stewed tomatoes + pasta = pasta primavera

Choosing Produce: Picking a Winner

Fresh produce is the key to a fresh-tasting meal.

This may come as a shock to those of you who've existed on frozen entrées up till now, but *fresh* produce doesn't come prepackaged. In fact, each variety comes in so many shapes, colors, and textures that you might be tempted to just close your eyes and point.

There are a few tried-and-true tricks for telling the good from the bad. Some fruits and vegetables show their ripeness visibly, while others get harder (or softer) or begin to smell better (or worse).

MOM SAYS: "You have to know what to smell, look, squeeze, and listen for."

1. **Sniff.** Broccoli, citrus fruits, melons, peaches, pears, and pineapples (sniff the bottom, not the tuft) should have a fresh, mild fragrance. Mushrooms should smell like fresh dirt. Fruits

should smell slightly sweet; a strong or sour scent can denote overripeness.

2. **Inspect.** Reject produce if it has cuts and bruises, and look for specimens with rich, healthy color and smooth skin. Strawberries shouldn't be too dark red or bruised. Most fruits and vegetables are at their best when they're glossy. Bananas, however, don't ripen until they're just beginning to show brown spots. Garlic shouldn't be sprouting; if it's green, it's bitter. Lettuce of every kind should be unwilted, with crisp green leaves and no signs of decay. Asparagus should have well-formed tips with no flowers sprouting from them.

3. **Squeeze.** Noncitrus fruits and squash should, in most cases, be fairly firm all over and free of dents or spongy spots. Ripe tomatoes should give just a little when cupped in your fingertips. Firmness in plums and peaches denotes immaturity; ripe specimens are less dense and more squishy. Citrus fruits should be heavier than their size would indicate; a heavy fruit is full of juice and ready to be squeezed or eaten. Avocados should be spongy when squeezed; if they're too firm, they aren't ripe. Grapes should come off the stem with a firm pull, easily, but not effortlessly. Onions should be firm throughout, with no telltale squashy sections.

4. **Thump.** A good melon sounds hollow and resonant, like a well-inflated basketball, when you thwack it. If it sounds more like you're slapping something solid, the melon needs to ripen.

Slow-Cooked Banana Bread

If your bananas get too ripe for your liking, don't throw them away—tuck them away in the freezer, and bake some banana bread.

Makes 1 loaf

- 1 cup (200 g) sugar
- 2–3 medium/large bananas (or 3–4 smaller ones)
- $^1/_2$ cup (114 g) butter, melted
- $^1/_4$ cup (60 ml) milk
- 1 tsp. (5 ml) vanilla

- 2 eggs
- $^1/_2$ cup–1 cup (50–100 g) chopped walnuts (optional)
- 2 cups (250 g) all-purpose unbleached flour
- 1 tsp. (5 ml) baking soda (not baking powder!)
- $^1/_2$ tsp. (2.5 ml) salt

1. In a large bowl, blend the first six ingredients listed. Cover with plastic and let the mixture stand until it reaches room temperature.

2. Heat the oven to 350°F (180°C).

3. Grease the bottom (not the sides) of a loaf pan, either 9" x 5" (22.5 x 12.5 cm) or 8" x 4" (20 x 10 cm).

4. Beat the banana mixture 1 minute on medium speed.

5. Fold in the nuts, flour, baking soda, and salt all at once, by hand, until just barely moistened. If you stir too much at this point, your bread will be a bit tough and chewy.

6. Pour the batter into your pan and bake for 50–60 minutes, or until a toothpick inserted in the center comes out completely clean.

7. Slide a butter knife around the edges of your bread, carefully flip it upside down onto a plate, and remove the pan.

Continue cooling for ten more minutes before serving. Mmmm!

Proper Chicken Protocol

Chicken is vital to good down-home cooking—but you have to handle it with care.

Without the taste of chicken, how would we describe the taste of everything else that tastes just like it? If you keep a stash in the freezer, you're always a quick defrost away from a tasty meal. It's the ultimate all-purpose food source: shredded, chunked, filleted, cooked whole or in whole pieces, chicken can be morphed into virtually any dish you can think of. But as Mom knows, buying and storing chicken can present some hidden dangers.

Fifteen to 20 percent of all chicken meat sold on the market is infected with salmonella, which can cause fever, vomiting, diarrhea, severe abdominal pain, and (very rarely) death in its victims; half of all commercially sold chicken is contaminated with a lesser-known microbe called *campylobacter*, which has sparked a well-chronicled but poorly publicized epidemic of infection in humans. Campylobacterial infections usually cause salmonella–like symptoms, which tend to be less acute—but it can spread from person to person for up to seven weeks after being contracted. The USDA doesn't even test raw chickens for this organism's presence, so it's up to you to protect yourself.

1. When you buy chicken, check the sell-by date. Growers aren't required by law to date their packaging, but sellers certainly are.

2. Your fresh packaged chicken should display no odd discolorations and should be cold (not cool) and firm when you touch it.

3. The grower's packaging should be tight and intact.

4. Before unpacking less perishable groceries, decide how and when you're going to cook your chicken and take the appropriate steps for safe storage and preparation. If you're freezing your chicken, make sure that your freezer is cold enough—0°F (–18°C) is ideal. The original packaging should be sealed inside a freezer bag or in a plastic container once the package has been opened (or if it's left in the freezer for more than two months). If you don't intend to freeze your packaged chicken, you should immediately refrigerate it at 38°F (2°C) and cook it within 24 hours.

Defrosting Tips

Never defrost chicken at room temperature. Instead, plan to keep chicken in the refrigerator for 12 to 48 hours to thaw before cooking it. (Boneless cuts will defrost overnight; whole birds and pieces can take up to two days.)

You can also thaw chicken in the sink—if it's still in its airtight freezer bag and the water is continuously cold (either keep it running over the container or change it every 30 minutes). Using this method, a whole chicken should take no more than three hours to thaw, and boneless pieces can take as little as 30 minutes.

The quickest way to get your frozen chicken ready for the cookpot is to microwave it on low power (most microwaves feature a well-marked DEFROST setting)—but be prepared to cook your meal immediately afterward, since the defrosted chicken might be cooked or warmed in spots when it emerges from the microwave.

5. When preparing to cook, establish a system for quarantining raw chicken: It should be kept far away from the other components of your meal—especially from foods that you'll be eating raw—and from any utensils and surfaces with which you'll prepare them. Reserve a special cutting board for chicken (preferably made of glass or acrylic rather than wood, which is porous and tends to collect bacteria), and scrub it with hot

water and antibacterial soap when you're finished with it.

6. Use a meat thermometer when cooking chicken. Stuck into a thick part of the meat, it should measure at least 180 degrees (82°C) for a whole bird and 170°F (77°C) for breasts.

7. Don't forget to scrub your hands and everything else that came in contact with raw chicken or your chicken cutting board.

Tip | Caution! Thanks to nature's ingenuity, salmonella can now infect hens' eggs without affecting the hens, so raw eggs can be the scariest food in your fridge. Eggs should never be stored in the refrigerator door, where they might get warm; instead, keep them in the back near the cooling element (remember, your fridge's temperature should be kept at 38°F or 2°C). Always cook your eggs *thoroughly*—if you're a fan of soft-boiled eggs or runny scrambles, you should think about changing your habits. And no matter how good that chocolate batter looks, never lick the spoon when you're baking.

Simple Chicken Marinades

Marinades are the easiest way to add zest to your chicken and creativity to your kitchen. Remember, a marinade improves over time—so plan your meal 48 hours in advance if you want your chicken to soak up all of the best flavors. Follow the suggestions below to complete three equally fantastic marinades or combine your favorite flavors.

1. **Soy sauce.** This is always a good beginning for a marinade, because it functions as a meat tenderizer. In a medium mixing bowl, combine a splash of olive oil with 1 cup (237 ml) of soy sauce, then add a clove of minced garlic, a teaspoon (5 ml) of powdered wasabi, a small piece of peeled and shredded ginger root, and 2 cups (475 ml) of orange juice. Mix into a runny paste, then coat your meat on both sides (use a pastry brush, if you have one). Cover the bowl, and put it in the fridge to marinate for at least an hour (and no more than 48), then remove the chicken and cook it to taste.

2. **Italian dressing.** Whether it's a creamy recipe or a more traditional vinaigrette, Italian dressing makes a wonderful stand-alone marinade. Pour enough dressing to coat your chicken in a medium mixing bowl, then add 1 teaspoon (2.5 ml) of black pepper and savory spices to taste. Marinate chicken as above.

3. **Dijon mustard.** Spoon enough Dijon mustard to coat chicken into a medium mixing bowl, then combine with a tablespoon (15 ml) of barbecue sauce and a dash of horseradish. For texture, try adding $1/4$ cup (45 g) sesame seeds. Marinate chicken as above.

How to Brew Tasty Coffee in No Time

Trendy cafés aren't the only places to get delicious coffee.

Before Starbucks, there was coffee. It just didn't taste as good. But have you ever really tried to brew a café-quality cup of java in your own kitchen? If you're still being served by the talented Mr. Coffee, it's time to try a new approach.

MOM SAYS: "Keep it simple, and you're guaranteed excellent coffee every time."

There are plenty of home espresso makers available, and they all make very good coffee. But if you can learn to live without the foam, buy a French press. This inexpensive piece of fully manual equipment can brew coffee so strong, rich, and flavorful, you won't believe you made it yourself.

1. First, buy whole beans. Invest in an inexpensive electric coffee grinder, and grind your beans as you need them (store the rest in the freezer to preserve their flavor).

2. "Pulse" the grinder for a few seconds only, so that the beans are reduced to a coarse but not powdery consistency.

Kitchen and Cooking Basics

3. Dump coffee into the press (figure one tablespoon [15 ml] of grounds per every cup [236 ml] of water), cover the grounds with boiling water, and stir to release and evenly distribute the coffee's flavors.

4. Once the grounds have been fully moistened, you can fill the carafe to the top.

5. Put the lid on the carafe and let the coffee and water steep for a few minutes.

6. Press down on the knob on the top of the lid so that the plunger is fully depressed. (The knob is attached to a round screen, which filters the coffee as it's pressed to the bottom of the carafe.)

7. Pour coffee into your favorite cup or mug.

Mom's Most Comforting Recipes

It's all well and good to live on a shoestring, but sometimes you need a little more Mom in your cooking. Enjoy each of these recipes by yourself or with a friend.

COMFORT TEA

1. Add 1 cup (236 ml) boiling water to fresh chamomile tea, and steep.
2. Add approximately 1 teaspoon (5 ml) of honey, $1/_2$ teaspoon (2.5 ml) of vanilla, and a splash of milk (vanilla soy milk is even better).

COMFORT COFFEE

1. In a French press, combine three heaping scoops of coffee and a teaspoon (5 ml) of cinnamon.
2. Fill the press with boiling water.
3. While coffee brews, warm approximately 1 cup (236 ml) of milk in a saucepan with honey. Keep stirring on low heat and don't let it boil or a skin will form. Pour the milk into a large mug.
4. Press the filter through the coffee, and add the coffee to the milk. For a sweet drink, proportions should be equal. For a stronger drink, reduce the proportion of milk.

GARLIC BETTER BUTTER

1. Combine chopped fresh garlic and water (in proportions of one part garlic to ten parts water) in a blender, and add a pinch of salt.
2. Blend until smooth.

3. Pour the mixture into a plastic container with lid, and put it in the freezer.

4. Give it an hour or two, and it will acquire the consistency of real butter. Spread it or melt it!

CUSTARD-FLAVORED SCRAMBLE

1. Beat two or three eggs in a bowl with a splash of water or milk, $1/2$ teaspoon (2.5 ml) of vanilla, and a pinch of sugar.

2. Throw in a pinch of salt and scramble in a lightly buttered skillet over low heat.

3. Sprinkle with mozzarella to taste.

SILVER DOLLAR PANCAKES

1. In a mixing bowl, combine ingredients for pancake batter as per instructions on the box.

2. Cut 1 large banana in slices.

3. Lightly spray your frying pan or griddle with nonstick cooking spray.

4. Put a slice of banana in the bottom of the pan, then pour pancake batter around it (not too much; the pancakes should be small). Repeat with as much batter (and banana slices) as can fit comfortably in the pan—leaving room for spatula maneuvering.

5. Wait until bubbles form on top of the batter, then flip the pancakes and brown the other sides.

6. Serve with plenty of maple syrup or the topping of your choice. (Try a scoop of ice cream for a truly decadent effect.)

The Art of Flipping Pancakes

All you need for successful flippage is a keen eye, an offset spatula, and several deep breaths to settle your nerves.

1. Pour a dollop of pancake mix on a griddle or skillet, and cook at a medium-low temperature.

2. Watch carefully as the batter starts to bubble around the edges. Wait until bubbles cover the entire surface and the edges start to lift and curl, and then get ready to flip.

3. With a steady hand on a sturdy spatula, take several deep breaths and slide the utensil in one swift thrust beneath the pancake.

4. Gently (but quickly) turn the pancake over, preferably without spreading or squishing the batter. The second side will cook nearly three times faster than the first.

BANANA FAJITA

1. Slice 1 large banana down the center.

2. Sauté both halves in a saucepan with a tablespoon (15 g) of butter.

3. On the griddle or in the oven, heat a soft corn tortilla.

4. Place the banana halves on the tortilla, and drench them in as much honey and cinnamon as you like.

5. Add a dash of fresh-squeezed lime juice, and roll the tortilla like a burrito.

6. Top with powered sugar, if you like it sweet.

STUFFED PEARS

1. Core a fresh pear; do not peel.
2. Place the pear upright in a baking pan.
3. Combine 2 tablespoons (30 ml) of brown sugar, a teaspoon (5 ml) of cinnamon, $^1/_2$ teaspoon (2.5 ml) nutmeg, and $^1/_2$ teaspoon (2.5 ml) cloves with $^1/_4$ cup (57 g) butter in a small saucepan.
4. Stir over low heat until the butter is melted.
5. Add 1 cup (225 g) chopped pecans (or walnuts) and mix until the nuts are coated.
6. Stuff the mixture into the cored pear, filling it to the top.
7. Bake at 350°F (180°C) for 30 minutes, or until the pear reaches the desired softness.

LENTIL SOUP

1. Soak a cup (225 g) of lentils overnight in a pot with a pinch of salt (use enough water to cover the lentils). Drain the water and rinse the lentils to remove grit, then set them aside.
2. Combine $^1/_2$ cup (118 ml) olive oil, half an onion (chopped or thinly sliced), and a clove or two of chopped garlic in a large saucepan.
3. Sauté the mixture until the onion turns clear.
4. Add the lentils to the saucepan and stir over low heat until mixture is well-blended.
5. Pour in a cup or so (236 ml) of water, and add $^1/_2$ teaspoon (2.5 ml) each of salt, pepper, and curry powder.
6. Simmer until the lentils are perfectly mushy.

BLACK BEAN SOUP

1. Soak 1 cup (225 g) of black beans overnight in a large pot with a pinch of salt. Drain the beans and rinse, then refill the pot with enough water to cover the beans.
2. Add a pinch of cayenne pepper, a pinch of cumin, and $1/2$ teaspoon (2.5 ml) salt, and bring the soup to a boil. Reduce the temperature, and let it simmer over low heat for an hour.
3. Add 1 sliced fresh tomato and half an onion (diced or chopped) to the pot after the soup has been simmering for 45 minutes.
4. Garnish with fresh cilantro and serve.

MUSHROOM CABBAGE SOUP

1. Pour 1 large can of chicken stock and 2 cups (473 ml) of water (or another can of chicken stock) into a large stockpot.
2. Add 2 cups (300 g) of raw pearl barley to the pot.
3. Cut in half a heaping handful of brown button mushrooms (add more or fewer mushrooms to taste) and shred a half head of cabbage; add to the stock pot.
4. Throw in several pinches of fresh rosemary and a pinch each of cumin and coriander (optional).
5. When the barley is soft, the soup is done.

SCRAMBLED SPAGHETTI

1. Cook spaghetti noodles, drain, and rinse in cool water (or use noodles left over from a previous meal—this dish makes a great midnight snack!).
2. In a separate bowl, whisk eggs (1 egg per measured serving of spaghetti; if you're hungry, use 2) with $^1/_4$ cup (60 ml) of milk and a pinch each of salt, pepper, and celery salt.
3. Melt a tablespoon (15 g) of butter in a skillet over medium heat and add the cooked noodles.
4. Stir-fry until the noodles are warmed and coated with butter, then add the egg mixture.
5. Cook for 5 minutes or until done, stirring frequently to properly scramble the egg.

DIRTY RICE (OR WHAT TO MAKE WHEN YOU'RE CLEANING THE FRIDGE)

1. Cook any kind of rice—brown, white, or wild—on the stove, as per instructions on the box.
2. While the rice is cooking, scavenge spoonfuls from nearly empty jars of salsa and taco sauce (or anything else that looks tasty) and shred or slice any leftover meats (chicken, ham, beef, pork); add them to the pot as you discover them—just remember to keep the pot covered when you aren't adding ingredients.
3. Slice a lime (leave the rind on) and drop in the slices.
4. Mix in your mix-ins as your rice is cooking. And remember, since some ingredients will have a high water content, they'll affect your

rice's cooking time. You'll have to wing it: Each time you remove the cover, stir the rice to check its consistency.

5. Your dish is done when the water is completely absorbed and the rice is neither too soft nor too dry.

Tip | When cooking rice, use the fingertip trick to make sure you have enough water in the pot. Once you've poured in the water, place the pot on a level surface and dip your finger straight in until your fingertip touches the top of the rice. The water level should reach the first joint of your finger—if it doesn't, add more water and repeat.

POPCORN WITH GARLIC DUMPLINGS

1. Coat the bottom of a large pot with olive oil, and spread popcorn kernels in a single layer.
2. Place fresh cloves of peeled garlic (as many or as few as you want) on top of the kernels.
3. Cover and cook on medium to low heat.
4. The treat is done when the corn stops popping.

Tip | Don't be afraid to eat the garlic cloves! They'll have the texture of dumplings, and a taste to die for.

Can't Miss Stir-Fry

What's the best way to keep stir-fried veggies crisp? Don't add 'em to the pan all at once. A perfect stir-fry starts with flavoring agents.

1. Coat a large, deep frying pan or wok with olive oil (just enough to coat the bottom) or spray with nonstick cooking spray.

2. Stir in a pinch each of your favorite savory seasonings (see next page for suggestions). For extra zing, try adding a pinch of powdered wasabi (but carefully—you don't want to overpower your seasonings).

3. Add hard, crisp ingredients like peppers, broccoli, snow peas, and carrots.

4. Add the semisoft group—mushrooms, zucchini, and other squashes—next.

5. Leafy or skinny vegetables like spinach, chard, bean sprouts, and cabbage go in at the very end, so they don't get soggy.

NEW GUACAMOLE

1. Peel, mash, and whip an avocado. Stir briskly with a large spoon, smoothing out the lumps as you go.
2. Add a squirt of lemon juice, a splash of soy sauce, 1 chopped habanero pepper, 1 chopped fresh tomato, a tablespoon (15 ml) of minced cilantro, and garlic to taste.
3. Add a pinch of salt and a pinch of pepper.
4. Stir well.

| Tip | **Instead of chips, try dipping with slices of sunchoke or carrot.** |

MASHED YAMS

1. Peel 1 large yam and chop in chunks.
2. Boil, drain, and mash as you would prepare mashed potatoes, adding a splash of milk, a tablespoon (15 g) of butter or margarine (substitute or add a tablespoon [15 ml] of olive oil for a different taste), and $1/2$ teaspoon (2.5 ml) salt.
3. With a large spoon, whip the yam until it's soft and creamy.

| Tip | **Meet the savory gang: Common seasonings like sage, thyme, and rosemary, along with bulbs like garlic and shallots, are often seen together in recipes. Each falls into the "savory" taste category—so if you ever need a reliable blend of spices, add two or three or all of the above.** |

Chapter 4: Housekeeping

Clean is a simple concept. It's also a simple goal. So why does the process of getting and keeping your house clean have to be so darn complicated?

For every task, there's a tool, a solvent, and a secret to learn. In addition, good housekeeping requires *infrastructure*: good habits, good organization, and strong resolve. If you build it, the rest will come—but not without some of Mom's magic know-how. Here's how Mom is able to do it all, without even breaking a sweat.

Meet Your Cleaning Agents

Three simple cleansers are all you need to make your home sparkle.

When you walk through the detergent aisle in your supermarket, it might seem as if you could fill a whole room, never mind a cupboard, with specialized soaps and cleansers. For any given surface, there are four or five soaps to choose from, each specifically developed (or so they say) to meet your surface's needs. And which is better? The foamy one, or the liquid one? The liquid one with New Fresh Scent, or the bargain brand that's cheap but stinky?

Now think back to that cupboard under the sink, in the kitchen where you grew up. Mom never seemed to use more than three or four cleansers, and some of these didn't even have labels.

To clean a whole house, you need a mild **abrasive cleanser** (which you scrub), a **nonabrasive cleanser** (which you rub), and **dish soap**—which tends to be marginalized as a kitchen-only item, but in fact can be used for a whole range of purposes throughout the house. Any other agent you desire can be mixed in various strengths from permutations of products you already have on hand, including vinegar, baking soda, and alcohol, plus a few it wouldn't hurt to buy—like ammonia and borax. Buy yourself a plastic bucket and keep some empty spray bottles handy for when it comes time to improvise.

Mom Says: "Know what type of cleanser is recommended for each of your surfaces."

1. **Abrasive cleansers** are good for scrubbing porcelain and stainless sinks, tubs, faucets, and stovetops.

2. **Non-abrasive cleansers** are what you'll use on just about everything else.

3. Good old **dish soap** is perfect for degreasing, spot cleaning, and stain removal.

For the abrasive, look for anything called "disinfectant scouring powder." This isn't a high-tech item—several of the best brands have been around for nearly half a century—so don't get distracted by fancy labels. The only key ingredient in any good scourer is a chemical compound (generally sodium carbonate and/or calcium carbonate) that tends to crystallize in rough, sandlike particles, which are excellent for scrubbing.

Tip | Mix your own abrasive by combining four parts baking soda with one part borax—or using either ingredient on its own. (Baking soda is also a great dry bath for dogs.) In a pinch, you can also use a pinch of salt! Just sprinkle some on your sink and countertops and start rubbing.

Nonabrasive cleansers come in many guises; you're looking for what's called an "all-purpose" agent. In this department, you're luckier than Mom used to be. The best all-purpose cleansers were developed for industrial use a scant 25 years ago, and they didn't hit supermarket shelves for at least another decade. Simple Green (or Orange, depending on your scent preference) is a nontoxic cleanser/degreaser that can be used on anything from crystal to cars. Applied at full strength or diluted with water, it does the job just as well as targeted products like tub and tile cleansers and antibacterial agents, as well as some of Mom's favorite solutions.

Given the effectiveness of all-purpose cleansers, you could probably forgo dish soap as an alternative cleanser if you had to, but then you'd definitely have to invest in rubber gloves if you intend to use the more heavy-duty cleansers regularly. Dish soaps have the handy ability to dissolve and remove grease from cookware without removing the natural oils from your hands—which means they're also good for cleaning fabrics, upholstery, carpets, and, in an emergency, hair. Vegetable-based liquid soaps are also an option, but they don't seem to be as effective as their synthetic counterparts.

Non-Abrasive Alternatives

If Simple Green isn't simple enough for you, there are several do-it-yourself all-purpose alternatives.

1. For a baking soda–based cleanser, dissolve $^1/_4$ cup (60 g) of baking soda in 1 quart (1 l) of warm water, or dissolve $^2/_3$ cup (158 g) of baking soda, $^1/_4$ cup (60 ml) vinegar, and $^1/_4$ cup (60 ml) ammonia in a gallon of warm water.

2. For a cornstarch vinaigrette, combine $^1/_4$ cup (60 ml) of white vinegar, 1 tablespoon (15 g) of cornstarch, and 2 quarts (1.9 l) of warm water.

3. Vinegar is also an excellent cleanser on its own. If you're cleaning to maintain and not reclaim—if, in other words, you're diligent about weekly scrubbing—you can use vinegar on just about anything that doesn't need scouring. Rubbed regularly on the inside of your oven, vinegar will keep it clean. Sprayed on shower curtains and bathroom surfaces, it will keep them shining and prevent mildew growth. (If you can't stand the smell, try adding lemon juice or orange peel.)

Borax, the Unsung Hero

Ask Mom, she'll remember: Borax was once the homemaker's hero. It could take the worst people-stains out of anything— erasing sweat, grease, bad smells, and honest dirt as if they'd never happened.

Discovered in Death Valley by the Borax Mining Company in 1872 and continually mined ever since, borax is a mineral that possesses an innate ability to deodorize and disinfect.

As a product, borax was marketed by the newly diversified mining company as the "20 Mule Team" detergent (borax ore was hauled by 20-mule teams), but it quickly found a variety of applications. If your shoes stunk, you sprinkled them with borax. If you had bad breath, you rinsed your mouth with home-brewed borax mouthwash. It deodorized clothes and sanitized bathrooms, and it wasn't even expensive.

So where did borax go? As it turns out, you can still find it in some stores in the detergent aisle, right where it's always been (if it's unavailable in your area, check the Internet). After its mid-century heyday, borax lost its audience to the trendier "bigger, faster, stronger" modern products. But there's no reason why it can't make a comeback—at least in your house. It's simple, nontoxic, cheap, and it works.

A Window into Window Care

There are many ways to clean glass, but not so many ways to get glass *clean*.

If you want to have spotless windows, you have to use just the right cleanser (to work on the tough grime), in just the right way (to avoid streaking), at just the right time of day (again, to prevent streaking). But what kind of cleanser should you use, and exactly how should you use it? And how do you get rid of that annoying linty residue?

To answer the last question first, don't use a rag. While some experts recommend using a clean, soft cloth, a crumpled newspaper will actually work best. The chemicals in newsprint apply a dirt-resistant film to the glass, and the paper won't leave part of itself behind, the way a linty rag will.

When it comes to technique, there are several tricks to attaining perfection:

1. Don't wash windows under direct sunlight, especially if it's hot. They streak when they dry too quickly.

2. If you're washing both sides of a window (and let's hope that you are), try using an up-and-down motion on one side and a side-to-side stroke on the other. That way, if you happen to end

up with streaks, you can tell which side they're on.

Mom Says: "Homemade window-cleaning solutions are even better than store-bought cleaners."

1. For moderately dirty windows, fill a spray bottle with warm water and a tablespoon (15 ml) of white vinegar. Spray windows, then immediately wipe clean. Polish off any leftover streaks with pure vinegar.

2. For extra-dirty or greasy windows, dilute $\frac{1}{4}$ cup (60 ml) of ammonia in 2 or $2\frac{1}{2}$ quarts (1.9–2.4 l) of water, load the solution into an empty spray bottle, then spray and wipe as usual.

3. For spot cleaning, use pure rubbing alcohol: Just daub on and wipe off.

4. If your windows are scratched, rub a little toothpaste (the paste kind, not the gel) into the crack, and polish with a cloth. You'll be surprised by the results.

When you're done, your windows will look as good as Mom's!

Get the Most into and out of Your Dishwasher

Always load your dishes properly to make the most of your dishwasher's cleaning capacities.

Dishwashers tend to be regarded with wary respect—and occasionally even fear. Many of us grew up with the notion that you had to pacify your dishwasher by washing the dishes in the sink first, or it would erupt like an angry god and vent its wrath all over the floor. But really all you need to know is what Mom has always known: how to load the machine properly.

MOM SAYS: "Put away those rubber gloves—and let your dishwasher do the dirty work."

1. Open your dishwasher door and make note of where the spray column rises from the bottom of the unit, through the middle of the bottom pullout rack. You'll want to be sure not to obstruct this area with pot and pan handles when loading the bottom rack.

2. Don't worry about scrubbing all of the food from your dishes before loading: Except for bones, bits of gristle, and any other hard detritus, your dishwasher is quite capable of flushing away residual traces of food.

3. Load the bottom rack front to back in this order: salad and mixing bowls, large dinner plates, and heavy pots and pans that won't block the spray column. Dirty surfaces should face downward, toward the spray arm.

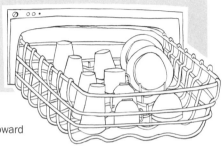

4. Flat items like cookie sheets fit well along the sides or back of the bottom rack; just make sure the soiled sides are facing inward.

5. The top rack is designed to hold lightweight plastic items, glasses, and smaller plates and bowls. If possible, wedge plastic cups and containers securely between heavier glass or ceramic dishes so they won't be flipped over by the spray.

6. Silverware should be loaded in the basket with business ends up and handles down (except for sharp knives, which should be pointed downward with handles up).

Oven Cleaning Made Easy

 Don't let your oven become a breeding ground for built-up grime—keep it clean!

Cleaning your oven range is a pretty simple task, particularly if you're a clean-as-you-go type. Simply wipe down your burners and surfaces with a wet sponge after each use. Every month or so, you can also remove the stovetop knobs and soak them in soapy water to dislodge any stubborn goo. Then it's on to the oven itself.

MOM SAYS: "Before you start to clean your oven, check the manufacturer's care label."

You'll need to determine whether your oven is a self-cleaning, continuous-cleaning or non–self-cleaning (standard) model.

1. Self-cleaning ovens feature a special cleaning cycle that can turn charred spills and grease spots into ash with frightening efficiency. Be sure to open the windows or turn on the fan to ventilate your kitchen while this cycle is running, because the fumes can discolor walls and surfaces. When it's over, simply wipe out the ash with a damp cloth and sponge the outside of your oven with dish soap or all-purpose cleanser.

2. **Continuous-cleaning ovens** have a special porcelain finish that can burn off adhered organic material at normal cooking temperatures. Maintenance is limited to a wipe-down (with a damp cloth) after the oven has cooled.

3. **Standard ovens** require quite a bit more care. You can avoid charred buildups by cleaning up spills as they happen and by protecting your oven's bottom with a cookie sheet. Every few months, you should remove grease spots by placing half a cup (118 ml) of ammonia in a warm oven and leaving it overnight (with the oven door closed and the heat off). In the morning, simply remove the cup and sponge off the residue with hot water and dish soap. If you aren't satisfied with the results, purchase a commercial oven cleanser and follow the printed instructions for use.

A Dust-and-Polish Primer

If you want your furniture to last, you need to know the do's and don'ts of wood maintenance.

Unless your taste (and budget) leans exclusively to glass and chrome, there's probably a lot of wood in your home. And thanks to Mom, the basics of wood care are probably already burned into your brain: always use coasters, never scoot a chair across the floor, wipe up spills when they happen, and don't water plants on the fine wood table.

But there's a whole world of wood care that goes beyond mere prevention. Maintaining the luster and beauty of your hardwood floors and furniture requires some special care.

Mom Says: "Regularly dust and polish your furniture so that you'll always be ready for company."

1. Always dust your furniture before polishing. Dusting once a week will keep your surfaces looking neat and will also inform you of any small stains or imperfections before they turn into bigger problems.

2. Be aware that the type of polish you choose to use at the outset will determine your choice in the future. If you start with wax, keep right on waxing—if you start rubbing oil into pre-existing wax, you'll create a sticky, caramelized finish.

3. Polish should be applied only three or four times a year; do it more often, and the finish will look cloudy instead of shiny.

4. Wash the wood surface as often as you like. Use a cloth dampened with dish soap or specially designed oil soap for regular cleaning.

5. Spot fixing should be done just as soon as you notice the spot: Rub toothpaste into water marks (with a rag, not a toothbrush)

to take them right out. Larger water stains can be removed by placing an absorbent rag or towel on top of the area, and then pressing it with a warm iron. To erase grease spots, try covering the grease with salt to absorb it and keep it from staining. To fix scratches, mix two parts lemon juice with one part of any kind of cooking oil and rub it into the blemish. Alcohol- and milk-based products can seriously degrade wood surfaces if spills aren't cleaned up immediately. Use a cloth dampened in lemon oil to remove alcohol spots and a cloth moistened in ammonia to clean up milk stains.

How to Dust

If you're not methodical about cleaning, you may quickly come up against one of the key conundrums of keeping house: If you don't start with the dusting, you're merely going to be rearranging dirt instead of cleaning it away. It's important to dust first so that you don't end up merely brushing dust onto all of the surfaces you've already cleaned (namely, your floors).

1. Choose your duster: A feather duster might be more fun to use, but an ordinary cotton rag will do a more thorough job.

2. Begin at the top of the room, dusting high moldings, the tops of window casements, picture frames, and any high surfaces.

3. Move on to lampshades and bookcase tops.

4. Now get into the nitty-gritty: empty your bookshelves one by one (again, starting from the top) so that you can clean each shelf individually before returning your books, pictures, and other objects to their respective homes.

5. Dust the surfaces of your coffee and side tables, making sure not to neglect the legs or any other carved work where dust likes to nest.

6. Finally, dust down all of your baseboards so that any accumulated grime is completely brushed away.

When applying polish to your furniture, the first thing to establish is not what kind of wood it is, but what kind of finish is protecting it. Soft, oil-based finishes require the use of oil-based cleansers for care, and hard finishes like varnish, lacquer, or polyurethane require another. It's often difficult to tell, just by looking, what sort of finish has been applied to your furniture. Virtually every type of finish is available in matte, semigloss, and glossy formulas, and the right treatment for one might damage the other. Newer furniture is often tagged with care instructions or accompanied by a care booklet—but if you're working with a vintage or antique piece, you're on your own.

Try a general-purpose wooden furniture cleanser/polisher on an inconspicuous corner of your piece. (These cleansers are available in oil- and wax-based liquid, cream, or spray formulas; some are marketed as scratch removers while others tout their capacity to shine, but they all have a similar overall effect.) If you're satisfied with the result, continue with the application. Make sure you follow the product's printed instructions about whether to use a wet or dry soft cloth, and whether to buff lightly or vigorously. Remember, most commercial polishes offer no real protection for the wood—so you still have to be careful about spills, rings, and dings. And if you've chosen a spray wax polish, you'll need to remove wax buildup every so often (when the finish starts to look dull or mottled) by cleaning it with liquid polish or by wiping it with a turpentine-dampened cloth.

If you want to get creative, you can mix your own polish from two parts oil (any kind of cooking oil will do) and one part lemon juice. Mix it in a spray or squeeze bottle; apply to wood with a soft cloth in one small area of the surface at a time. To avoid streaks, buff in tight circles rather than in a linear, back-and-forth motion, and dry with another clean cloth.

| Tip | **For sweet-smelling homemade polish, try using a few drops of essential or scented oil instead of cooking oil, or adding a pinch of lavender or rosemary.** |

MOM SAYS: "Don't treat your hardwood floors the same way you treat your wood furniture."

1. Do *not* use furniture polish on your hardwood floor unless you're very good at ice-skating. Check the label on most commercial wood furniture polishes and you'll find a note warning you of excessive slipperiness; it's best to take this seriously.

2. Thoroughly sweep your floors with a stiff broom that is capable of reaching into corners.

3. Brush the collected dirt into a dustpan and into the trash.

4. Mix a weak solution of one part vinegar to four parts water in a bucket for everyday cleaning. Use an old-fashioned rope mop to spread the solution across the floor—if you use a self-wringing mop, you'll have to dry the floor afterward with a towel. (Self-wringers often leave spots of standing water, which can warp the wood over time.)

5. For a more stringent cleaning, use Murphy's Oil Soap (follow instructions on the bottle) or a turpentine-based liquid cleaning wax. If you're using the latter, make sure you open all the windows and turn on the fan.

6. Every couple of months, be sure to brush out the joints between your floorboards. A long-fibered brush is best for the task, but in a pinch you can also use a toothbrush.

Caring for Your Marble and Stonework

Marble, slate, and ceramic surfaces need special care.

Marble is, indeed, a rock—but as rocks go, it isn't very hard. Grit tracked in on your shoes can abrade it, and the acid in vinegar can damage it, so if your hardwood floor in one room shares a seam with the marble in the next, be extra careful with that hardwood vinegar cleanser.

MOM SAYS: "There's a right way and a wrong way to clean every surface."

1. Marble should be washed with warm water and dish soap and dried immediately afterward so that the water does not soak in and leave spots.

2. Tough stains can be treated with ammonia and hydrogen peroxide. Add a few drops of ammonia to a small container of peroxide, and apply the solution to the marble.

3. Cover with plastic wrap and seal with tape or weights, then leave it overnight.

4. When the cover is removed, sponge off the mixture and buff the area dry.

5. For a very stubborn stain, try a gentle abrasive: rub the surface with a damp rag and baking soda. If your removal process leaves a dull spot in the marble, wet the area, rub a bit of tin oxide–based polishing powder into the spot, then buff it dry with a thick, soft cloth.

6. Once clean, your marble should be polished with a tin oxide–based marble polishing product (found near the wood furniture polishes and cleansers in most stores).

7. For cleaning tile and slate, use nothing but plain warm water. These surfaces incorporate a sealant-coated grout, which should never be scrubbed with oil- or acid-based chemicals.

8. The grout between tiles should be cleaned about once every two weeks with a sponge or toothbrush and a mid-strength solution of hydrogen peroxide and water (one part peroxide to four parts water)—but if you clean your grout frequently enough, you might not even need to use chemicals at all. Try rubbing the grout with a typewriter eraser, and you might be surprised by the result. For deep cleaning, rub straight peroxide into the grout with a rag or a sponge, cover it with plastic wrap so it doesn't evaporate, and let it sit overnight (or until you can see that the grout has whitened to your satisfaction). Soak up excess peroxide with a sponge when you take the plastic off.

Tip | If your grout is colored, don't clean it with peroxide—unless you want to turn it white!

Tip | Top-quality stone should never be touched by an abrasive. If the stain is particularly bad, call in an expert experienced in marble care. Ask a marble importer/retailer for an expert recommendation.

Keep Your Vacuum Sucking

Don't forget to change your vacuum cleaner bag regularly.

Back and forth, back and forth, ten, fifteen, twenty times . . . and you're still trying to vacuum up that piece of thread that's coyly curled on your carpet! Clearly, your vacuum is experiencing a weakening of suck-power.

There's an easy solution to this problem: simply change your vacuum cleaner bag. Even if the bag doesn't look or feel full, its opening might have become clogged with fine dirt or dust, and it's time to remove the old bag.

If your vacuum came with a manual, read the instructions to determine which bag to buy. If it was purchased second-hand, check the packaging of available bags (at supermarkets or hardware stores) to match your vacuum's make and model with a compatible bag.

Once you've acquired the proper bag, it's time to remove the old one. Most bags attach to the vacuum via a cardboard disk that securely surrounds the opening. Lay several pages of newspaper on your floor and place your vacuum cleaner in the center so that any residue falls on the paper. Gently pull back on the disk to dislodge it, dispose of the dirty bag, and replace it. (Once it's installed, the new bag should look just like the old one—only empty.)

With or without a new bag, a vacuum's power can be greatly affected by sucking in inappropriate objects—so make sure your floor or surface is free of all coins, paper clips, thumbtacks, nails, rubber bands, and large pieces of string or thread. If your vacuum accidentally ingests any of these items, turn it off immediately and unplug it before reaching into the rotating brush to remove the debris.

Tip | **String can be especially irritating to your vacuum, because it winds around and around the brush once it's swallowed, and generally results in an acrid burning smell; if you don't remove it immediately, it can snarl up and damage your vacuum's motor fan.**

Sympathy for Your Sofa

The best way to protect your upholstery is to take good care of it from the get-go.

If you were lucky, you had a crazy great-aunt who wrapped her couch in plastic and didn't let you lie on it without taking off your shoes. If you weren't so fortunate, that plastic-coated couch was in your house—and Mom was its protector.

There's a reason why Mom and sundry old ladies take extreme measures to guard upholstery. Some fabrics can be treated with fabric guard to help repel stains, but such treatments can only help, they can't heal. They also can't be used at all on fabrics with a nap, including velvet, suede, or chenille (or anything else soft or fuzzy). Leather, suede, and many fabric blends don't hold up at all to home cleaning.

Mom Says: "Read the care label before attempting to clean your sofa.

If you check under or behind your sofa, you'll probably find a tag that says S, W, S/W, or X.

S = solvent (dry-cleaning) only
W = clean with water only
S/W = clean with either solvent or water

X = don't clean at all—just brush it down

If you happen to have a W or S/W item, clean it carefully. Don't just squeeze some dish soap on a rag:

1. Add one part soap to four parts water and whip it in a bowl, using a spoon or a blender, until dry suds form on top of the liquid.

2. Dip a soft-bristled brush or rough rag into the suds and rub it into the fabric. If you are simply cleaning the sofa and not treating a stain, you should test a swatch of fabric on the back of the sofa where any changes in color will be less noticeable.

3. If the soap seems to be producing good results, clean away. But don't expect magical results: some types of stains—especially if they've been there a while—are simply beyond the power of dish soap. And some fabrics won't tolerate soap at all: If the spot you've been rubbing gets discolored or faded, or if it seems to shrink or change in sheen or texture, you'll need to have the piece professionally dry-cleaned. (Note: Professional upholstery cleaning is never cheap, only moderately effective, and occasionally deadly to upholstery. You'll need to find a company that specializes in your sofa's particular kind of upholstery, and hope for the best.)

If the experts can't save your sofa, you have three options: reupholstering, finding a suitable slipcover, or making a phone call to the Salvation Army.

Fighting Mold and Mildew

 Common sense and weekly cleaning can do wonders for your bathroom.

Mildew is a subgroup of fungal mold, which inhabits the air in spores that can settle and grow on virtually any surface, moist or not (dampness merely hastens colonization). If you block the initial forays of mold and mildew, they'll never be able to build a flourishing culture.

MOM SAYS: "Show mold and mildew who's boss."

1. Open the window when you shower, even if the air outside is chilly, or install a ventilating fan. All of that steam has to go somewhere, or it'll condense on bathroom surfaces and accelerate the growth of mildew.

2. After you're finished showering, wipe down the walls or spritz them with a vinegar, water, and lemon juice cocktail (two parts water, one part lemon juice, one part vinegar). If the vinegar/lemon scent is too overwhelming, use a commercial after-shower spray.

3. Spray the shower curtain or door, as well as the walls inside your shower stall. No rubbing or scrubbing is required—just

spray it on and leave the mixture to dry.

4. When the fungus manages to break through—in the grout, if nowhere else—use straight bleach (or a watered-down solution, one part bleach to five parts water) rubbed on with a tooth-brush or sponge, or use a scrub brush with a commercial cleanser that features bleach as a main ingredient or additive.

5. Let the bleach solution soak for a bit, then scrub with a toothbrush.

6. Rinse with the same solution, and then repeat until the grout is thoroughly clean.

> *Tip* **When using bleach, be sure to put on your rubber or latex gloves (and a mask, if you have sensitive nasal passages). Open the bathroom window so that you have sufficient ventilation, and—if you've already been cleaning with a different agent—rinse the affected surfaces with water before applying the bleach. NEVER use bleach with another cleanser.**

Bleach-sensitive people can use an all-purpose cleanser or a strong abrasive as alternatives, but the end results will be questionable. New stains will recur easily, and old ones tend to be stubborn even in the face of energetic scrubbing. (If you can't come into contact with bleach, be sure to scrub the very first time you see the black stuff invade your shower or tub.)

Cleaning Your Toilet Bowl

The best way to clean a toilet is through prevention.

One simple preventive measure will reduce the need for heavy toilet bowl cleaning: Pour chlorine bleach into your toilet once a week, let it sit for a few minutes, and then flush it away. Alternatively, you can use a scrub brush with an all-purpose cleanser (three or four good squirts should do the job) or cleansing powder to scrub the bowl's entire surface once a week; make sure you lift the lid and poke your brush into all the nooks and crannies under the rim to clean and unclog the water jets.

If you can't commit to weekly therapy, your toilet will need to be cleaned periodically (e.g., twice a month) with an anti-bacterial formula that is strictly marketed for toilet bowls, or you may need to install a continually cleaning in-tank cleanser. If you choose the ongoing in-tank solution, your toilet should be flushed at least once a day—otherwise, bleach will stand in the tank and begin to degrade its parts.

| Tip | **Don't forget to change your in-tank solution! If you're wondering whether it's time, put a few drops of food coloring in your toilet bowl and watch them for a minute or two; if they don't fade away, the bleach in your cleanser is spent and it's time to replace the unit.** |

Mom's Guide to Fabric Care

Good fabric care is worth the time and effort.

Machine wash, tumble dry are four of your favorite words. Perhaps you've tried the "put 'em in, spin 'em around, and wear what comes out alive" approach to laundry (which does, if nothing else, keep the process simple)—but there's always room for improvement. The key is to know your fabrics and the extent of abuse they can take.

Polyester. Polyester is 100 percent synthetic. Technically, it's categorized as an oil—so polyester garments tend not to "breathe" very well. On the upside, they wash and dry nicely, pack well, and don't wrinkle, shrink, or fade. ***Washing instructions:*** Machine wash (hot for whites, warm for lights, cold for darks); tumble dry.

Rayon. Rayon is the product of a natural fiber and a synthetic process. Modern rayons are sturdier than their vintage counterparts—which should always be dry-cleaned—but it's still risky to launder them at home. Rayon shrinks a bit every time you wash it, so keep this in mind if your clothes are tight fitting. ***Washing instructions:*** Dry clean only; hand or machine wash on delicate cycle (cold temperature) if you want to risk it; hang dry.

Silk. Sometimes, there's no need for innovation. As it has been for more than a millennium, silk is still spun by fat, pampered silkworms. And although it's generally woven into lightweight materials, silk preserves body heat just as well as wool does. If it's stretchy like a stocking, silk can be hand washed. And some silk fabrics are actually designed to be washable (and are generally labeled as such). As a rule, however, silk should be dry cleaned; colors fade and some weaves get "crispy" in water. (Tip: If you're tired of taking silk scarves, ties, and other accessories to the cleaners, try washing them in cold water with shampoo formulated for chemically colored hair.) **Washing instructions:** Dry clean only; for stretch weaves, hand wash (cold temperature); hang dry. Some silks will require ironing; make sure you set your iron's dial to the proper setting.

Wool. Wool is produced by a variety of sheep and sheeplike animals and can be woven in a wide variety of textures. It's very warm, frequently itchy, and generally dry clean only. Several wools and wool blends on the market are labeled as "washable," and indeed, they are—but as a rule, unless the garment's printed care instructions are actively inviting you to wash it, you should play it safe and take it to the cleaners. Never, never put a wool garment in the dryer. (If you do, you'll have some marvelous doll clothes on your hands.) ***Washing instructions:*** Dry clean only, except for washable wools; washability will be indicated on your garment's care tag.

Linen. Linen is a natural fiber spun from flax. It's lightweight and airy to wear—but it wrinkles like a paper bag. There is no such thing as nonwrinkling linen: some weaves look less wrinkly than others, but all linen creases when you sit on it or crumple it in a suitcase. ***Washing instructions:*** Machine wash (cold temperature); hang dry. Get out the elbow grease when you get out the iron: linen usually comes out of the wash in a crumpled wad and requires a substantial commitment to the ironing board to make it look presentable.

Cotton. You already know why you like cotton: it's light, breathable, and extremely comfortable against your skin. Some heavyweight cottons, like denim or canvas, come out of the dryer like new, while shirt-weight weaves need to be ironed—whether you hang them to dry or not. For the most part, cotton will shrink when you wash it. Loose, open weaves tend to shrink more than tight weaves (like denim or canvas), but you can count on your cotton garment (unless it's preshrunk) shrinking at least 10 percent in its first washing. Some cotton voiles (netlike, transparent weaves) and jerseys will shrink by close to a third. ***Washing instructions:*** Machine wash (hot for whites, warm for lights, cold for darks); tumble dry (loose, open weaves should be hung). Iron as you see fit, especially if you want a crease in those khakis.

Stretch weaves. There are two types of stretchy fabrics: jersey (a T-shirt–type material that stretches in all directions) and Lycra-added blends (which stretch only one way when pulled, like stretch jeans). Jerseys can be made out of virtually any-thing—wool, cotton, poly, silk, you name it. On the other hand, Lycra, in 2- or 3-percent quantities, is generally added to cotton, polyester, or wool to form one-way stretch blends. Except for wools and wool/Lycra blends and some special exceptions (any blend incorporating metallic or acetate threads; read all tags carefully before taking the plunge), most stretchy fabrics are washable. Cotton and polyester jerseys (i.e., T-shirts) can go in the dryer, but Lycra blends should be hung to dry; Lycra can either shrink up or lose its stretch in too much heat. ***Washing instructions:*** Machine wash (hot for whites, warm for lights, cold for darks); hang dry (except for cotton and poly jerseys, which survive nicely in the dryer).

Sorting Laundry: The Keys to Success

 Sort your washable clothes carefully to avoid soap streaks, lint, shrinking, and discoloration.

When Mom used to do your laundry, did your clothes ever shrink or fade? Not likely. Mom knew that that best way to extend the life span of your clothing was to make the extra effort to launder your different fabrics separately. This may have seemed like a world of mystery to you as a child, but the basics are actually quite easy to master.

MOM SAYS: "Be sure to choose the right temperature and cycle when loading your washing machine."

1. Sort your laundry into four piles: whites, light colors, darks, and heavyweight fabrics.

2. Make sure all pockets are empty, and zip up loose zippers. Turn dark pants inside out to prevent the color from bleeding or fading.

3. Add soap to the washer (follow product instructions) and select the appropriate water temperature. Darks should be washed in cold water, lights in warm, and whites and heavyweights in hot.

4. Next, select your cycle—most fabrics can be washed on the regular setting, but use the gentle cycle for delicate garments.

5. Start the washer and allow the detergent to dissolve before adding a cup of bleach (if desired).

6. Now add your clothes. Don't overfill! Clothes should be gently placed—not jammed—around the agitator in an even layer; an overloaded washer won't efficiently remove dirt or rinse soap from your clothes.

7. When the cycle is finished, check the care instructions before putting garments in the dryer (some should be hung to dry, or dried flat). And don't forget to empty the lint trap!

Tumble at Your Own Risk

In 1998, the National Fire Protection Association reported the annual number of dryer fires averaged 14,800 between 1993 and 1997—that's 40 fires a day. Annually, neglected dryer lint causes an average of 14 deaths, 307 injuries, and $75.2 million in property damage in the United States alone.

Why? When lint accumulates in the duct beneath your dryer, it causes the motor to overheat. Volatile lint trapped under the dryer is sucked by the updraft into the duct, where it sets fire to the clumped particles of dust and fabric. Cotton and polyester—particularly polyester—burn viciously once they've been ignited, and are extremely difficult to extinguish. In order to prevent these fires, dryer manufacturers and servicers agree with Mom that lint traps should be checked before every load and emptied after every load.

Major appliance manufacturers have created an arsenal of brushes, vacuums, brush-vacuums, and vacuum-brushes designed specifically for eradicating lint from your lint trap. Regardless of which tool you use, it's important to brush the trap *gently*—if you puncture or tear the filter screen, you're opening a whole new can of fire hazards. After brushing or sucking the offending particles, make sure that the lint trap slides completely back into place.

It's also a good idea to clean the whole dryer duct once a year.

Damage Control: Mom's Best Stain Removal Tips

You don't need fancy stain removers to get stubborn spots out in a jiffy.

Stains are difficult to avoid—unless you happen to have eyes in the back of your head and a couple of extra hands. But even if Mom didn't come fully equipped with extra eyes and hands (it only seemed that way to you), she somehow always had just the right trick up her sleeve when the time arrived, no matter how stubborn the stain.

MOM SAYS: "The right solution and a little elbow grease will take common household stains out in no time."

Coffee or tea. To eliminate stains from countertops or mugs, moisten a tablespoon (15 g) of baking soda with water—get it just wet enough to form a paste—and rub it over the stain with a rough sponge. If unsuccessful, rub the stain with a damp rag and a few drops of chlorine bleach, or soak the mug overnight in a solution of 2 tablespoons (30 ml) of chlorine bleach per cup (236 ml) of water (and rinse well with warm water before drinking out of it again).

Bathroom or kitchen soap scum. Vive la baking soda! Used as a damp paste (as above) or as a scouring powder right out of the box, baking soda can take care of any soap residue. Rinse with plenty of cool to lukewarm water after application.

Hard water spots. Apply equal parts vinegar and lemon juice to affected areas on sink tops and faucet fixtures, and let the solution sit for a few minutes. Rinse with cool to lukewarm water and buff affected surface with a rag. Repeat if the stain persists, this time allowing the solution to sit a little longer.

Urine (from all animals). Soak up as much of the urine as you can with paper towels (they absorb more efficiently than cloth), then scrub the spot with sudsy dish soap and a well-wrung sponge. Blot the excess moisture with paper towels, then rinse with a low-strength solution of vinegar (one part vinegar to four parts warm water) applied with a spray bottle or daubed on with a rag or sponge. Tear off three or four paper towels and place them in layers over the stain. Weigh the towels down with a couple of books, and let sit overnight (or for a full day). The stain should be gone when the books are removed. Vacuum or scuff to blend the area into the rest of the rug.

Grease. Depending on the placement and severity of the stain, one of three solutions should work. If the grease is on upholstery or a wood surface, pour salt on the spot. If the stain is very recent, the salt will absorb the grease and can then be vacuumed or brushed away. If this technique isn't successful, try abrasion. (Caution: Do not try this method if the fabric is labeled "dry clean only.") Use a rough sponge dipped in dish detergent (and well wrung out) to rub gently until the spot disappears. If this last technique isn't successful, repeat the abrasion method, this time using a wad of steel wool.

To remove grease from clothing, pour Coca-Cola straight onto the stain, agitate the area by hand, and let it sit for a few minutes while you sort the rest of your laundry. By the time you've put the rest of your load in the washer, the stained garment should be ready to throw in. Add your regular detergent and wash according to the fabric's instructions.

Chewing gum on fabric. Separate out the egg white from a single egg and pour it on top of the gum. Use your fingers to work the white into the gum until it comes out completely. Rubbing the gummed surface with ice cubes (or, if it's feasible, putting the whole object in the freezer) is also a good removal method. Once the frozen gum hardens and cracks, you can pry the pieces up with your fingers.

Tip | The egg white method is definitely the most effective way to remove gum from hair.

Wine. The key to treating any sort of wine stain is immediate action. For spills on washable fabrics and upholstery, pour salt on the spill to soak it up (or blot it with a cloth) and sponge the spot with warm, carbonated water so that the bubbles lift out the stain. Rinse the item for three or four minutes in hot running water (or keep sponging it with hot water, if you're cleaning a piece of furniture), and then wash it according to the fabric's washing instructions.

For carpets and nonwashable materials, the watch phrase is "pat—don't rub!" Use a sponge or a damp rag to blot the stain—first with carbonated water, then with dish soap, and then plain water. If your carpet or garment is white, you can also use a whitener, such as hydrogen peroxide, or—for magical results within seconds—chlorine bleach. Soak a cotton ball in water, add a few drops of bleach, and squeeze to wring out the excess moisture. Now daub the stain with the cotton ball, and watch it disappear. Immediately wash the bleach out to avoid spotting.

Tip | **Bleaching should be reserved for truly white fabrics only. It will leave a snow-white spot on off-white or dyed garments.**

Blood stains. The key to removing bloodstains is temperature: if you heat a bloodstain in order to clean it, any residual discoloration will be permanently set in the material. First, blot the upholstery or carpet with a cold, damp sponge, or rinse the stain in your garment in the sink with cold water. Then, use hydrogen peroxide straight from the bottle to blot and then flush the stain from a garment, or simply blot the peroxide with a rag or sponge if the stain is on carpet or upholstery.

Pressing to Impress

Ironing can improve the appearance of nearly any garment.

Perhaps you've avoided buying an ironing board because, deep down, you really just don't relish the task of ironing your cotton and linen pants and shirts. Buy one anyway: an ironing board is a relatively inexpensive investment that will make your ironing experience much more efficient and satisfying.

MOM SAYS: "Make sure there's a method to your ironing."

1. Check to see which heat setting is appropriate for your garment. If you're working with cotton or linen, it will probably need to be steamed, so fill your iron with distilled water before you turn it on. Cottons and linens require the highest heat; wools and cotton blends take medium heat; and polyesters, rayons, silks, and acetates require low heat.

2. When ironing shirts, follow a plan. Start with the collar, ironing the back and then the front. Iron cuffs next (inside first). Lay sleeves flat and smooth out any creases, then iron them on both sides (back side first). Iron front panels one at a time, from shoulder to hem, then turn the shirt over to iron the back.

Your shirt will be slightly damp when you're finished, so hang it immediately to avoid further wrinkling.

3. To iron pants, first turn them inside out. Iron the waistband, pockets (both sides), and fly, then turn the pants right side out. On the pointed end of your ironing board, iron the right side of the waistband and pleats (fit the pointed end into each pleat in order to fill it and smooth it out). Lay the pants lengthwise on the ironing board, with any permanent creases lined up. Fold the top leg up to reveal the inside of the bottom leg, then press the bottom leg. Turn the pants over, and repeat the process for the second leg. Then, move the bottom leg aside and fold the top leg down so you can press the outside. Repeat for the second leg. Fold the pants carefully over a suit hanger (or hang them from the waistband with clothespins) to prevent them from wrinkling.

Sewing 101: Mom's Basics on Buttons and Hems

Save time and effort by making repairs and alterations at home.

As with most ventures, the first step to learning the sewing basics is acquiring the right equipment. Drugstores and supermarkets stock pocket-sized emergency kits, but that's all they're really good for: emergencies and pockets. So make the pilgrimage to your local fabric store. You'll be able to pick up some basic supplies, plus new buttons to replace any lost ones.

MOM SAYS: "Sewing on buttons takes no more than ten easy steps."

1. Make sure you have enough light to see the thread against the fabric without squinting. It's easy to make mistakes in dim light. (It's also easy to mistake black thread for navy blue, or vice versa.)

2. Choose a thread that's as close to the color of your garment as possible.

3. Thread your needle, pull the thread through the needle until both ends are even, and knot the ends together. (You can either roll the threads in your fingertips to blend the strands

and then knot them or tie them twice like shoelaces.)

4. Place the button where it belongs on the garment.

5. Make the first stitch from below, poking the needle upward through the material and one of the holes in the button. (Your knot will end up on the inside, where it can't be seen.)

6. Pull the thread until it's taut, and then poke your needle downward into the next hole, all the way through the material, until the thread is again taut.

7. Repeat this process about six times, or until you're satisfied that the button is secure. You'll finish with your needle in the reverse side of the fabric.

8. To tie your finishing knot, make a tiny stitch through the material, but do not pull the thread through all the way. Leave a small loop, and pass your needle through the loop once or twice before finally pulling it tight to form a knot.

9. Repeat the knotting stitch once more, just to be safe.

10. Cut the thread close to the knot, and you're finished! (Don't forget to stick your needle back into the pincushion so you don't step on it later.)

MOM SAYS: "There are several ways to hem pants: Mom's way, and every other way."

Mom's way, of course, is the best.

1. Use your seam ripper to carefully rip out the existing hem and unfold it.

2. Place each pant leg flat on the ironing board, and iron out the crease from the original hem.

3. Put the pants on and slip on the shoes you intend to wear with the pants. (The right length for socks is often way too short for shoes.)

4. Take off the pants. If the legs are more than an inch (2.5 cm) too long, cut off the excess. Lay each pant leg on a flat surface and cut straight across. If the pant legs are extra-wide, you might want to measure the amount you're going to cut with a ruler and mark it on each side of each pant leg, to make sure that both pant legs are the same length all the way around. Make sure that you leave the legs about an inch (2.5 cm) too long, so there's enough fabric to turn up for a hem.

5. Turn the pants inside out and put them on again. Fold the edge of one leg up so that the edge end is even all around and the length looks just right.

6. Pin the edge in place with one or two straight pins in the front or on the side, to mark where the length should be. Then, carefully remove the pants.

7. Using the first pins as a guide, pin the folded hems all the way around each pant leg.

8. Use a ruler or measuring tape to make sure that the hems on each leg are the same width, so you don't get one leg shorter than the other.

9. With the pants still inside out, iron the bottom of each leg to form a sharp crease. (If your straight pins have colored plastic heads, don't put the iron directly on top of them—they'll melt!)

10. Now, choose an appropriate thread—the color should closely match that of your garment, and if possible, the thread content should match the fabric content.

11. Thread your needle, tie the securing knot (as on page 143), and keep the pants inside out so that the pinned, folded edge

is visible and easy to work with. Make a small stitch to begin your hem.

12. As you're stitching, keep checking to see how the hem looks on the outside. Seen from the inside, each stitch should be about one-third of an inch (1 cm) apart, but from the outside, the stitches should be nearly invisible. (Make sure that each time your needle emerges on the right side of your pants, you reinsert it in almost the same place.)

13. When you finish each pant leg, remember to tie off your finishing knot on the inside.

14. Enjoy your new pants!

Chapter 5:
Love and Relationships

If you're looking to learn about the ways of *modern* romance, rent a movie—don't ask Mom. If Mom had her way, you'd handle love like a biohazard (slowly, warily, and zipped from head to foot in plastic).

But even though Mom may not know much about your generation, she still has a pretty good track record when it comes to the basics of looking for love, finding love, and letting love go. Ideally, you'll be lucky in love, but in the meantime, you should be smart enough to remember Mom's best advice.

Preparing Your Date Uniform

For a special occasion, steer clear of The Special Outfit.

When you really care about looking especially good for a date, you might be tempted to try a little too hard to project a look that may not be "you."

Example: After shlepping through every chic boutique in town, you've purchased an ensemble that's absolutely unlike anything you've ever worn before. New color, space-age fabric, new cut: The thing is an essay in engineered asymmetry. Unfortunately, it makes you feel like a lopsided rhino. And just like that, there goes your evening. You can smooth, adjust, unbutton, and untuck, but that rhino will not be tamed.

The same advice applies to both men and women: Stop trying so hard. If you aren't comfortable in your clothes, you'll feel self-conscious, and you won't be able to project the real you.

MOM SAYS: "If you want to dress to impress, wear something tried-and-true."

1. Leave the risqué clothing in your closet, at least on the first date. Tight pants or a plunging neckline may come off as more intimidating than appealing.

2. By the same token, "tried-and-true" does not mean knock-around sandals and your favorite jeans. There should be a clear indication, expressed through your personal style, that this outing is a special occasion.

3. Your clothes should be just-washed clean, and not only-wore-it-to-a-movie clean. You can dress up jeans with a button-down shirt, or dress down good slacks with a T-shirt. Above all else, be sure to pay attention to your shoes (women do, especially). Whether they're new and stylish or worn and classic, they should always be clean and polished.

4. Dress appropriately for the venue or occasion. Even if the destination is supposed to be a surprise, your date should give you a general idea of what's suitable and what isn't. (Otherwise, you might find yourself at a dude ranch in a silk suit, or at the opera in khakis and a T-shirt.)

5. If you must wear new shoes, scuff the soles to head off any unfortunate spills. You can rough up the soles on cement before trying to walk on carpet or give the soles a couple of quick rubs with sandpaper.

6. Don't wear an investment item. If you're worried about the welfare of your incredibly expensive, impossible-to-clean designer jacket whenever it's draped over your chair or stored under your seat, you won't be able to focus completely on the more crucial aspects of your date.

Fashion Don't   *Fashion Do*

Love and Relationships

Listening Isn't the Same as Hearing

If the person you're dating is worried that she's going to hurt you, she will.

In terms of time spent, dating is more about talking than . . . well, *not* talking. People say a lot when they're getting to know one another. But in a romantic context, each conversation is a sales pitch in disguise. Behind every anecdote and true confession lurks the specter of *agenda*.

Let's say that the first few dates have passed the test and you're moving on to a more serious phase of commitment. Your date sighs deeply, stares intently into space and says, "I'm afraid I'm going to hurt you." To which you, of course, respond with pity for her tortured soul and needless fears of failure. Wow, you think. How sweet.

Well, consider yourself warned. This

particular statement should *not* be written off as romance-induced rhetoric. What it means is that your partner either has problems with commitment in general or with commitment to you, specifically—and that her fears for your emotional safety are probably well-founded.

MOM SAYS: "Actions may speak louder than words, but sometimes people really do mean what they say."

Here are a few common phrases that should raise a red flag.

1. I just got out of a relationship, so I'm not looking for anything long-term.

2. I'm really bad at commitment.

3. I don't think men and women were meant to be monogamous.

4. Let's not make any promises.

5. Why put a label on what we have?

6. Even if we do this, we're still going to be just friends.

7. I was so busy, I didn't have a chance to call.

8. You won't always love me.

9. You deserve someone as special as you are.

If the person you're dating expresses any of these not-so-subtle hints of ambivalence, get the message: she's not ready for the long haul, and you'd do best to cut your losses while you can.

There's No Such Thing as "Can't"

"I'm sorry, but I just can't explain it." Sound familiar? "Can't" is generally a vague, unjustified (or unjustifiable) "won't"—a handy way of passing the buck to some decision-making force of nature. If you won't do something, you have to explain why you won't; but "can't" lets you off the hook—or does it?

In the context of a relationship, saying "I can't" is like slamming the door in your partner's face. It's a great way to avoid discussing the real issues and feelings that may be causing problems or misunderstandings to arise. But remember, the more frequently you shut that metaphorical door, the more likely it is that your partner will shut a real one—behind her, when she leaves. If you really want a relationship to work, cut out the "can'ts" and have a real discussion.

Recognizing Love When You See It

Falling in love is the easy part.

Now that you know the warning signs that tell you a relationship may not have potential, how can you be open and aware enough to recognize a relationship that *will* work?

Mom Says: "The hard part is making something out of *being* in love."

Wise people like Mom will tell you that sometimes there's no substitute for experience on this count, but a relationship that has the potential to last is usually one that has at least two of these characteristics:

1. You've found a person who makes you feel relaxed and confident and excited all at the same time.

2. You're compatible in your tastes, hobbies, and habits, as well as in your communication skills.

3. You contend with stress and adversity in similar ways. For instance, if you tend to avoid drama, solving problems as they arise, but your partner seems to thrive on strife, you may want to be wary. But if you're in tune more often then not, even when

the chips are down, you may have found someone with whom you are truly compatible.

Sex Is Not Always a Many-Splendored Thing

Don't give it all up at once.

Yes, it's true. If Mom had her druthers, you would never give it up—to anyone. Unless, of course, he could provide you with at least two personal, professional, and psychiatric references, an impeccable credit report, and a list of (recent) lab results that proved him to be free of any communicable diseases. And even then it would be a bad idea, unless it came with a tangible sign of commitment, courtesy of Tiffany's.

Nevertheless, in the real world, sex happens. And pretty frequently, Mom turns out to be right: Under a lot of circumstances, it is a bad idea.

What goes wrong? Despite many myths to the contrary—going all the way back to the Bible—sex is not a shortcut to love. If employed as a way to gain someone's love, it's often a shortcut to broken dates and unreturned phone calls.

Shakespeare had it right: "What's won is done. Joy's soul lies in the wooing." If you use sex as a trump card, you might discover that you and your partner are playing very different games. For you, the game might be "How to Close the Relationship Trap on Someone I Really Like," while your partner is honing his skills at "How to Get Someone Cute into Bed."

Sex is a universal language, but everyone speaks it differently. And unless you and your new love are speaking the same dialect, you can count on being stumped by mis-communication.

Mom Says: "Why would anyone buy the cow when you can get the milk for free?"

If you're looking for commitment, especially of the perma-nent, legally witnessed variety, the transaction has to have a hook. In terms of sex (which is, after all, the real focus of Mom's advice on this subject), this would translate into keep-ing your zipper up until the "I do's."

But there are all kinds of perks and intimacies, beyond the physical ones, that *also* should not be bestowed on an undeclared, potentially undeserving partner before you've given it some serious thought.

1. **Understanding and reciprocity.** Before offering your partner your unwavering devotion, you should be very sure that your partner

is committed enough—and capable enough—to reciprocate. Otherwise, you're just being useful—and if you're not careful, you may find yourself frustrated by a one-way relationship.

2. **Intimacy and affection.** You should be able to turn to your partner as a reliable source of cuddles, reassurance, and support. He or she should be the kind of person who can be nurtured and is not afraid to nurture you in return.

3. **Logistical and financial support.** Do you want to be a patron or a partner? It's extremely painful, not to mention expensive, when the person you've bankrolled and supported through good times and bad turns traitor and deserts. Combining your financial assets with your partner's can be a risky proposition (sometimes even within the confines of marriage). And committing your checking and savings accounts to someone who's still uncommitted . . . Well, that's love at its blindest. Simply put: Don't do it. Wait to see whether your relationship will have the staying power to go the distance, and in the meantime, take pains to ensure that dates, trips, and vacation expenses are evenly shared.

Why would anyone buy the cow when you can get the milk for free?

Break It Down to Avoid Breaking Up!

Most couples would agree: Money is the root of (nearly) all evil when it comes to maintaining a healthy relationship. A perfectly happy duo can erupt into name-calling if someone neglects to pay a bill and the phone gets disconnected, or if someone else just had to buy that $300 pair of shoes. There are several ways to cut down on this sort of unpleasantness.

1. Both partners must have a realistic sense of their combined total income and an agreed-upon picture of the lifestyle that it can (and can't) support.

2. The couple should know where their respective paychecks are deposited—in each partner's individual account, a joint checking account, or in some agreed-upon combination of the two—so that one partner's "play" money doesn't get earmarked as bill money by the other.

3. Partners should itemize their household finances. List every utility bill, credit card bill, rent, loan, mortgage, insurance, and car payment that must be made on a monthly basis, and decide on the account that each bill will be paid from and whose job it is to pay it. Be realistic! If one partner tends to be irresponsible, don't expect him to change overnight. Instead, put him in charge of less vital transactions.

Prioritize Your Outrage

You can't win all of the battles, all the time.

You can't even fight all of the battles, all of the time. Anger takes a lot of energy to sustain: No matter how many things upset you over the course of a relationship, getting equally upset about all of them simply dilutes the impact of your indignation when it's really good and righteous. It also dilutes your credibility—once you've developed a short-fused reputation, your reactions and opinions are immediately suspect.

MOM SAYS: "Love is an ongoing negotiation."

You have to decide what you're willing to give up in order to get what you really want. Know your priorities.

For instance, if your partner doesn't ask how you're doing at work, you might read it as disinterest, while she simply wants to give you privacy. Or if your partner forgets Valentine's Day, you might read it as thoughtlessness—but don't forget that he brought you flowers last week. Some people just aren't holiday oriented, but they're romantic on their own terms.

If you get outraged whenever your partner fails to treat

you "right," and if you find yourself getting outraged all the time, you have three choices.

1. Understand that some part of you actually enjoys being outraged, and love your partner even more despite those things you perceive to be "inadequacies."

2. Let go of your fairy tale, and get to know and accept your partner as a real person. Adjust your expectations and avoid the outrage.

3. Opt out. If, while pursuing choice 2, you discover that your partner's view of what's right is dramatically, dangerously different from your own, put an end to the relationship in the most mature way possible: by finding a mutually caring and amicable way to part.

How to Argue Properly

If you and your partner tend to explode at the drop of a hat, it's time to agree on some rules of engagement so that you can plan for the inevitable future arguments.

1. Never start an argument unless you—and your partner— are willing to concede from the outset that the other person might have a valid point.

2. Pick a lull in the fighting during which you can both sit down and talk. At this time you cannot bring up the grievances that cause your fights to occur. You're not going to discuss who started it, who doesn't fight fair, or who misses the point. You're just going to focus on the process.

3. Establish this safe-and-sane rule: If either party notices that the discussion is escalating into an argument, he or she can and shall cut it off before it becomes a full-blown fight. How? By simply refusing to escalate the argument any further: Just stop—right in the middle of a sentence, if you have to. This cessation shall not be interpreted by the other party as a forfeit or concession of defeat. It shall simply be regarded as a pause.

4. Both parties should take a deep breath. You can agree to continue the discussion later, when you regain the ability to communicate reasonably.

Would You Rather Be Right or Be Happy?

Admitting you're wrong isn't the same as admitting you've lost the battle.

Throughout human history, millions have died trying to prove that they were right. For some folks, it seems like the only thing better than being right is fighting about it.

Arguments over being right always seem to devolve into the bitterest bouts of name-calling and accusations. So when the next big Right Fight happens, take a minute to think. What are you really fighting about?

MOM SAYS: "Being in love means having to say 'You're right.'"

The need to be right often boils down to the need to assert your independence. If you've been feeling trapped in your relationship, or if you feel you've gotten the short end of the stick once too often, you may find yourself passionately insisting that two ottomans are otto*men* or that the wedding last weekend started at three-*fifteen*, *not* three o'clock.

Chances are, your relationship is having power problems that should be addressed and not channeled into pettiness. Try to be aware of what you're really frustrated about. If you

and your partner are bickering too much, here's a handy trick
for changing the tide: Try saying, "You're right." It's hard to pick
a fight with someone who is trying to see your point of view.

Never Go to Bed Angry

Put arguments to rest before your head hits the pillow.

How many loves have been lost to insomnia? You're never
more alone with your pain than in the nights when you're
lying right next to the person who caused it. You're left all
alone with your grievance, which is potentially as explosive
as dynamite.

Without someone arguing to the contrary, it's easy to
nurse a small grudge into an angry bull. Inevitably, your focus
begins to shift to other grievances . . . and that bull becomes a
herd, just itching to stampede.

In every relationship, there's a sleeper and a stewer. If
you're the stewer, you've spent plenty of nights replaying your
arguments and perhaps even plotting revenge. If you're the
sleeper, you're familiar with the mornings that follow, when
you're startled awake by strange accusations or silently and
mysteriously shunned. It's like waking up with Kafka.

Going to bed angry is bad for both partners, and it's

certainly bad for a relationship, no matter what the cause.

MOM SAYS: "Save the stewing for the crockpot."

1. If your argument is dragging into the wee hours, be the first to call a truce. Simply say, "Let's stop right here, and talk about this tomorrow after we both have had some rest."

2. Remind yourself that your partner really isn't evil—more likely than not, one of you has simply hit a raw nerve and you'll be able to talk about it more rationally when the heat of anger wears off some.

3. Take some nice, deep calming breaths, and try to think about the *good* things you share with your partner.

4. Don't start pushing buttons after prime time. Generally, the topics of your arguments aren't time sensitive—so you can choose when to open the forum for debate and secure yourself a good night's sleep in the meantime.

Don't Go Changing

To thy own self be true—especially when it comes to relationships.

If you're like most people, you're a slightly different person with each of your friends, since each relationship requires you to display different aspects of yourself. You're funnier with your funny friends, smarter with your smart friends, and badder with your bad friends.

It's only logical that your best relationships are the ones in which you like yourself the most. If you have to try too hard to be scintillating, if you find yourself making lifestyle choices with which you aren't comfortable, or if, for whatever reason, you start to behave dishonorably, you may want to take a hard look at the relationship and the person you become within it.

Mom Says: "Don't do anything that you—at your best—wouldn't do."

Sometimes, in the context of a relationship, you'll adapt so much that you become another person altogether. And disturbingly enough, you may feel more comfortable playing the role of this new person than you do your unadulterated self.

For a variety of reasons—low self-esteem, fear of failure, and other insecurities—it's very easy to fall into the role-playing trap. Not the naughty kind of role-playing, but the psychological sort.

Ask yourself the following:

1. Do you need to feel like the hero?

2. Do you like playing the helpless princess?

3. Are you only happy when you're the existentially anguished prince?

These roles are seductive because they're familiar, and you know exactly how these fictional people would behave and react. That gets you out of the responsibility of reacting honestly, and of making carefully considered choices. You don't have to think, just follow the script!

The worst aspect of role-playing is that your relationship becomes a story with an old, familiar ending. You've hired a fat lady, and she's waiting in the wings. The only surprise, at this point, is when she's going to waddle out and lament the tragedy.

It's easy to fall into this trap. Many people aren't happy

unless they're being hurt, while others aren't satisfied unless they're defending someone who needs their help.

Give up the drama! Until you stop playing a role, you won't find a happy ending.

Que Sera, Sera—Translated

If he breaks up with you, he wasn't the right one anyway.

This is one of Mom's favorite platitudes. She's convinced that you're the best thing on the planet and that if someone can't see that, the problem is theirs—not yours.

Her logic seems so patently untrue. But you have to admit that Mom has a point. Relationships are built on love, trust, and compromise, yes—but they're also built on a shaky foundation of egos and expectations.

Attraction isn't just about chemistry; it's about whether someone lives up to a certain image that you have in mind for a significant other. It's about whether this person's résumé of skills, experience, intellect, style, body type, hair color, and so forth fits your ideal and your needs.

And so, all pheromones (and hormones) aside, the dating process can basically be reduced to a series of interviews. If someone else gets the job, it's not because you weren't qualified, but because his or her particular skill set was more suited to the position available.

So Mom's right: If it didn't work, it wasn't meant to be. And you can thank your lucky stars that you didn't get the job.

Relationships Require Lots of Heavy Lifting

Once you've made your bed, keep it made.

You've shopped around. You've rented. You've leased with an option to buy.

And now, finally, you've decided to put your money where your heart is and make a permanent commitment—be it marriage or some other sort of long-term arrangement that puts you and your partner together for good times and bad.

But what will make it work? What will make it fail? And how will you know what the limits are?

According to Mom, there are some major conditions that cannot be tolerated in a committed relationship—like abuse and adultery—but hundreds of reasons for remaining committed to your commitment.

Living in constant proximity to anyone is bound to be boring, frustrating, and downright infuriating at times. And like everything else, a committed relationship is subject to the laws of entropy: if you don't actively hold it together, it will come apart. It takes work. It takes discussion. It takes negotiation.

Once the bloom has worn off, think a few more times than twice before deciding you've made a mistake. Take steps to renew your relationship from time to time. Be spontaneous and go out on a date if it's been a while since you've been out on the town.

Above all, don't forget about all of the things that you still love about your partner—and remember to tell her about them as often and as earnestly as you can.

If you really need a fairy tale, try this one: The frog becomes a handsome prince. The prince and the princess get married. They buy a house, a DVD player, and a really comfy chair, and bang! He turns right back into a frog, and she turns into a shrew. And the frog and the shrew grow so old and wrinkly that you can't tell them apart. And they both live happily and irritably ever after.

Index

Acknowledgments

This book is an homage to Bob and Maude Fayer, who know 98.9 percent of everything.

Thanks must go out to my Pocket Team: Some were born patient, some learned patience, and some had patience thrust upon them . . .

To Liz Lazich and Ace, Eric Andruss, Tea Leaf Green and household, Jay Vallon and Brendena Houmari, Peter Froehliche, Jill Jensen, Jimmy Robinson, and my friends at Britex Fabrics for their help with discipline and distraction; to Candace Bridges for the recipes and encouragement; to Mom Simon for the Mom-away-from-Mom advice; to Heidi Hungerford for daily writer maintenance (featuring her famous slow-cooked banana bread and Barb Hungerford's scrambled egg spaghetti) and help with the manuscript; to Octavio Rojas for proofing and quoting me back to me when it counted; to Richard Klein for making The Phone Call; to my editor Mindy Brown for her talent (and for not shooting me whenever I missed a deadline); and to Roger W. Reinitz . . . for everything.